GRAND PLANS: HOW TO MITIGATE GERI-DRAMA IN 20 EASY STEPS

Susanna P. Barton

Grand Plans

CONTENTS

PROLOGUE

TOTAL RELIEF IS THE way I feel most days. After five years and innumerable hours of stressful thought, I finally closed my eyes. I cut the last ties to a prolonged caregiving fiasco by shutting down the final physical reminder of it — a mini-storage full of junk. It's all gone now — the bills, the emails, the reminders, the pressure of the stuff. The whole Gordian Knot experience has been snipped free and is now roly-poly pell-mell tumble-bumble in the rearview mirror, getting smaller and less cataclysmic by the minute. Gah... it's such a sweet relief. It's done. It's gone. It is freaking over.

Total relief is also how I feel about both my parents being gone, though the relief I feel about their absence is washed in sadness, regret, and nostalgia. I miss them. I love them and am grateful to have known them as my parents. But weirdly, I am glad we don't have to look toward their future through the lens of anxiety, illness, or impairment. I feel fortunate not to face those kinds of fears anymore. Call me a crazy, but I'm relieved.

I look around now and see peers with parents going through some challenging, devastating stuff. They are making tough financial, medical, and legal decisions — they're playing the dreaded "What If?" game like their lives depend on it (which it does, by the way!), and they're exploring all the realms of senior care, living, and management that will make any sane person's head spin 50 million different directions at once. They're wondering what to do with all that stuff in the house and garage — in the GD mini storage. If you're a Gen Xer, this is your story! And if it isn't yet, I promise it will be one day soon.

And here I sit, strangely relieved. I still have two parents-in-law rocking life like they're 18 and Life to Go. But somehow, they feel like "someone else's" responsibility at the end of the day. Because they are, actually. Mine are now — gone. Poof. Relief? I'm not even sure that's the right word. It's a complicated feeling.

My thoughts have turned to myself and how I can make life easier for my children and theirs. My relief has reminded me how much work I must do to prepare. It's time to get my shit together. It's time to make sure my kids have a play book. It's time to recognize I, too, will die. It's time to gather and leverage the experience we all have and the certainties. It's time for a Grand Plan.

Introduction

I HAVE SPENT THE past few years in turmoil over what I can do now to make sure I am an educated, well-prepared, exceedingly loving, and infinitely self-aware older person down the road. You probably feel the same way if you have ever managed a difficult elder care situation or muttered to no one WTAF(??!!) about a loved one's life planning choices.

It's called geri-drama. It's what happens when older loved ones – perhaps even older loved ones named you or we – refuse to consider the realities, complexities, and contingencies of aging. If you know, you know. Geri-drama is the worst, geri-drama is denial, geri-drama is a shitty thing to do to a loved one. Geri-drama is the WOAT – the worst of all time.

I'm talking about those eye-roller moments at the family dinner table when the geri-person you love says something like, "I'm not old," or "I plan to age in place," or "I don't want to talk or even think about it" in answer to any legitimate query about their senior planning. Or maybe it's go-time during some out-of-the-blue crisis (which is nearly always the case), and your person has NO PLAN – financially, medically, legally, or otherwise – to expect, acknowledge, address, or much less fix the problem. This worry flares up if your loved one refuses to hand over the keys, allow in-home assistance, or have honest conversations about end-of-life care. Maybe they skedaddle over to the realtor's office and buy a three-story home with lots of steps and tons of stuff...or worse, a puppy. And you're standing there like, OMG, because you know precisely how these choices will affect you and others in your sphere one day. And you think – perhaps you harumph audibly – "I will never do this to someone I love!" These are the times when you start designing a better vision for your senior experience. These moments should inspire the Grand Plan in all of us.

My journey in grand planning began 30 years ago when my mom passed away unexpectedly at 51. I was just 20 and at the height of college misbehaving, with zero experience adulting, so my brother and I lingered quietly on the sidelines. In contrast, our sweet dad drove all the "clean up" and processing and headaches the passing of a loved one usually includes. I observed these hardships and weathered some intense personal sadness, but always from a safe emotional and tangible distance. One thing I noticed during that time was the addition of a new and increasingly LOUD internal stopwatch that began tick-tocking away after my mom's death – one that continues ticking away today. As my own 51st birthday loomed on the horizon, I thought about my mortality more and more. I expected death to come my way soon and swiftly. This stupid stopwatch informs my grand planning to this day.

But nothing prepared me for – read, scared me into – grand planning more than the caregiving situation I mentioned earlier – management for an elderly couple in South Florida in 2018. They were the mother and stepfather of a childhood friend who died tragically 10 years before. My friend was the only child of an only child of an only child. The family was practically nonexistent in this situation. Unbeknownst to me and my father, my friend's mother had named us their Power of Attorney and trustee should she or her husband be unable to manage their affairs. And it's a good thing they had planned so well legally and named someone, even two people as seemingly random as my father and me, because when we got involved, the wheels were falling off their life bus – like <u>every</u> wheel, on <u>every</u> side, at the <u>same</u> time.

I started getting cryptic calls and worrisome messages from their housekeeper about unpaid bills and unsafe living conditions – and worse. I learned this couple had begun a sad, slow spiral into a desperate situation. One was nearing end-stage Parkinson's and could barely communicate or get out of bed. The other struggled with dementia and alcoholism. Neither could care for themselves, much less the other person. They also had a big dog, three houses that someone could have easily featured in TLC's "Hoarders: Buried Alive," dwindling finances in multiple, difficult-to-access accounts, and legal drama from many angles – including their HOA, which wasn't about to let their too-high-hedges and unkempt landscaping go, even for a minute. The power was turned off a few times. One house was four days away from foreclosure...because that's what happens when you don't pay the bills or taxes. That's what happens when you let stuff go.

It was a shit show of epic proportions. And since, at the time, my near-octogenarian dad was hands full with his own life in the wilds of northern Mississippi middle-of-nowheresville in his great big house with mounds of period furniture and extra cocktail napkins, I stepped in with about zero experience in geri-care to help right their sinking ship. I was so unprepared it was painful. But I quickly learned how to fax POA documents and manage home healthcare, hospice support, home-selling, and – holy hell, the stuff! The horror of the stuff! – and purging it all! Trying to figure out how to pay for all the plus, plus, pluses associated with a no-wheeled bus/water-filled boat. Four years later, I'm still feeling PTSD from it.

Then, Dad died in 2021, and I embarked on my master's in death coping and grand planning. I doubled down on hospital experiences and funeral preparations, legal drama, and more stuff purging – the party bags of corn chips, the multiple sets of Pier One tableware, the books, the jackets with unpopped TJ Maxx tags, the fake Civil War-era belt used for "staging," the pennies – God, the coins!! – the elegant and massive collection of books, and the like. Though I felt somewhat more prepared for this work, both mentally and practically, I still felt pissed. Pissed that this grand-planning stuff was an under-the-radar, little-discussed life education. I was pissed at everyone who had already gotten their higher death degrees for not revealing helpful truths or sharing honest conversations. Pissed and full of wonder that so few people are willing to talk about this like normal, life-experiencing, everyday aging adults.

I am not the only pissed, frazzled, unrepentant person out there. My experience is shared. Research from the national caregiving firm A Place for Mom indicates that in 2020, 41.8 million Americans were providing unpaid care to adults over 50 – that's 17 percent of the U.S. adult population, folks. That's a freaking LOT of people doing really hard, out-of-the-goodness-of-your-heart kind of work. A July 2022 University of Michigan National Pool on Healthy Aging confirms this statistic. The study found that 54 percent of respondents report helping older adults over 65. Of that group, 65 percent indicated significant challenges to the role, including emotional or physical fatigue, balancing work or other responsibilities, lack of time for self-care, and balancing time with family and friends.

Sadly, the worst is yet to come. According to a February 2020 report from the U.S. Census Bureau, all Baby Boomers will be over 65 by 2030 – marking a demographic turning point for the United States. In 2016, there were 49.2 million people 65 years or older (15 percent of the population), and by 2030, that number is expected to be 73.1 million, or 21 percent of the population. Jump to 2060, and the population estimate for people 65 years or older climbs to a staggering 94.7 million people. That's nearly a quarter of the U.S. population! And here's the kicker: Generation X caregivers and geri-drama-experienced are part of this illustrious and expanding group. Any adult in this very moment will be one day, too.

The tragedy, as I see it, is that most people in this demographic – particularly the Baby Boomers who will all be over 65 come 2030 – have not packed very well for their senior stroll, the very one we should all see coming. I doubt many folks have even discussed it. The perils and potholes of old age are inconceivable to most older adults until they stumble into one on a clear and beautiful day. And that's when they realize not only are these liabilities furreal, but they are also expensive – sometimes too costly or too far gone even to remedy.

A May 2022 study from Fidelity Investments published on CNBC.com showed that a 65-year-old retired couple in 2022 will spend an average of $315,000 in healthcare and medical expenses during their retirement. And that's not including the big expense nut: caregiving and long-term care services. According to the AARP's Long Term Care Cost Calculator, which determines average care costs and options in zip codes across the United States, the average monthly cost for 24-7 in-home personal care services in my community is nearly $17,000. The monthly cost for residential care housing options in this zip code is significantly less. Still, it is significant nonetheless: the average monthly cost of an assisted living center option is $4,660. In contrast, a semiprivate nursing home bed costs $8,212, and a private nursing home costs $8,881 monthly, the AARP calculator shows. If my poor math skills are correct, that's $204,000 yearly for 24-7 in-home care and $106,572 a year roughly for an assisted living center situation.

Most normal, average, everyday people don't have this kind of money just sitting around for a rainy day. But we should. This unseen financial and health crisis on literally everyone's horizon is the single most important event of our lives. It's all been forecasted and calculated, folks. We cannot escape this destiny! We cannot "fix" it, sidestep it, or pretend it's not happening. But we can do something to prepare for it: talk about it. We can anticipate it. We can embrace thoughts like "What can I do now to ensure this doesn't happen to me and the people I love? How can I learn from all this BS and be all the better for it? How can I leave a better legacy for my family?"

That's how my grand planning obsession evolved. And I'm pretty sure this unfolding is familiar to you, as well. After my personal encounters with elder planning "don'ts" and out of total desperation, I started stirring up conversation through an online community called Grand Plans. I discovered many intelligent people out there have gone through excruciating senior care scenarios, and they are quite willing to talk about it – some with great enthusiasm, authority, and understanding. And if you want to see the absolute darkest side of caregiving on social media, join one of the caregivers' group pages where people describe everyday horror stories with sad regularity. It makes your heart feel melted and super disturbed. And I guarantee all these people feel the same sense of resolution to do it better, smarter, and more lovingly for their children. Once you've been through the proverbial ringer with this geri-stuff and know how negatively it can affect loved ones, you are determined to change the course for yourself and others.

So what if the 69.6 million Baby Boomers ahead of us were terrible at real talk senior planning or making solid end-of-life plans? That doesn't mean all the Gen-Xers coming along – all 65.1 million of us in the United States alone – must follow suit. Our legacies have more potential than that! If you've ever been crushed by the responsibility of propping or cleaning up an older person's life, you know there absolutely MUST be a better plan – a set of best practices, steps, or pro-tip strategies – to kicking ass and taking names on that sunset stroll.

Turns out there is! However, more people should be talking about it.

Through conversations with geri-experienced friends on Grand Plans' social media pages and podcasts and via work discussions I began having as part of Jacksonville Mayor Donna Deegan's subcommittee on local eldercare issues, some common threads of that perfect Grand Plan began to emerge – adding to and underscoring what a few other brave writers, observers, and geri-realists have been putting out there into the world recently. While everyone has their unique experience navigating the Golden Years with their aging loved ones, the fundamentals of a Grand Plan are highly standard. This is excellent news because it means the steps toward gold-star senior living are well paved.

So, after listening to others and learning from my own experiences, I discovered there are about 20 steps we can all take now – earlier than most of us think is appropriate – to significantly reduce geri-drama during our Golden Years. These inputs are based on shared stories and reflections – from people I know and books I've read. Together, these 20 moves form a Grand Plan that guarantees reduced stress for the loved ones who will one day be our caregivers, organizers, or life managers. Take even one step of this Grand Plan, and the future looks brighter. Take at least 10 steps, and your golden years are truly golden. According to multiple conversations, interviews, and research, I believe the fundamental action items for designing a workable Grand Plan are to take the following nine concrete steps and supplement them with 11 soft steps, which I break down in greater detail in the following chapters:

Concrete Steps – the "Musts"

- Make lists of everything essential and create a 'death binder.'

- Pen your obituary and plan your funeral objectives.

- Hire an attorney to get legit about your affairs.

- Get your financial house and plan in order.

- Write your prescription for health, hope, and hospital issues, and consider your medical thresholds.

- Educate yourself on the cost, scope, and reality of the geri-life you envision – particularly your residence.

- Minimize the hell out of yourself and your stuff.

- Consider pet acquisitions carefully.

- Relinquish the keys and be ready – eager even! – to be a passenger.

Soft Steps – the "Shoulds"

- Embrace your age, appearance, and role.

- Focus on your mind, body, and soul.

- Communicate with your people early and honestly – and often.

- Trust the people who love you.

- **Establish, build, and stay connected to a reliable, loving, accessible community – pick "your person or people."**

- **Be relevant and keep up with key technology.**

- **Invest resources in younger generations, service, and others.**

- **Play the "What If" game constantly and get mentally prepared.**

- **Play "Ask Yourself, Honestly," and plan authentically for your future.**

- **Be realistic, open, and flexible.**

- **Design a legacy that you'll be proud of, and practice empathy, humility, and gratitude.**

It bears repeating: If you can accomplish, discuss, or consider at least a few – even ONE – of these 20 objectives on your approach to the sunset stroll, I promise you will shine and be shown great appreciation and affection by your people. You'll also feel the peace of doing something brilliant for yourself and your people. Only good comes from honest conversation, realistic planning, trust, compassion, and empathy for others – this is the truth!

The fact that EVERYONE has to deal with this cannot be understated. Nor can the number of people who don't have a reliable network to fall back upon. Sometimes options 1,2,3 and 4 are not available. You simply MUST have a plan – several of them.

I'm not the only middle-aged weirdo making outrageous promises about grand planning. Many other writers, scientists, doctors, and ordinary people concur with this boiled-down-for-Golden-Years success. I share a few of my favorite findings throughout the book.

I've been blogging, podcasting, and promoting authentic dialogue about these critical ingredients for the past year. Seeing a simple, workable Grand Plan emerge from so much prior confusion, anger, and annoyance has been cathartic. These conversations elicit amen after amen after AMEN! It's not that hard, folks! We can do it if we're conscious of it, and I hope this book of "steps" will encourage you in this important life journey. Think of it as a book of reminders with which you can one day whack yourself on the backside or hold up in front of the readers you can't find. If experience is any measure, people must remember to be realistic, conversational, and pleasant about these topics. Half the battle is just being committed to the remembering part of a Grand Plan.

Decline is real, folks! Make your Grand Plan part of your long-term memory. Recognize that one day you may not remember, you may not understand or you may not be fit to make a good decision.

Grand Plans: How to Mitigate Geri-Drama in 20 Easy Steps will be that book of reminders for you as you set out on your grand planning work. In this collection of essays and experiences, you will hear me and other experienced, ordinary people BEG you to do so.

The 20 steps are organized into chapters, which include a definition of the problem, a solution to the problem, and a list of resources that may help the reader better approach, understand, and manage the problem. I've avoided being too process-oriented or directive, but I am keen on sharing real talk that motivates people to improve their situation. The goal is to talk about ways to be more self-aware and prepared for our Golden Years – the actual how-to is up to you, my friend.

However, once you sit down with some of these experiences, it's clear why we must normalize the thinking around it. If you love the people living life with you, around you, and in the generations behind you, show them you mean it by preparing a workable Grand Plan.

Unless you are some looney tunes who enjoys causing your loved ones' emotional distress, there is significant work we all need to do to find and promote peace during our sunset stroll. This peace comes from good planning, presence, contentment, community, and compassion. These reflections will help you and your loved ones rise to new occasions with reality and connection at the forefront. Welcome to your future Grand Plans!

Part I: Concrete Steps — the "Musts"

Step 1: Make lists of everything important, create a 'death binder'.

THE PROBLEM, IN REAL **talk:**

When you're dead or are unable to manage your life anymore, your loved ones are going to have a freaking tough time shutting things down or getting a handle on your affairs if you don't have it all written down somewhere easy to access – like in a death binder or something similar. Smart, planful, organized people make death binders. But most people don't. This is a shame and causes the living major headaches and ermagahs that attach to and sour your legacy.

When I became "the person" for that unrelated-to-me couple I mentioned in the introduction, my first role was playing Sherlock Holmes. I hired a private financial manager recommended by their attorney, and we spent months revealing and untangling the details of their financial, medical, and legal organization (or lack thereof!) before we could get busy lining up the most appropriate support. This involved many faxes, snail mail, excessive notary paperwork, and WTAFs. Honestly, it was not easy, and I would not wish it on my worst enemy.

The solution IMHO:

Whether it's a manilla folder full of papers, an organized binder of cataloged information, or a digital file or email, a "death binder" or collection of pertinent information is something you need to start assembling NOW – before there's a crisis and before you forget it's essential.

Funny sidenote – a friend was telling me how relieved she felt to see that her uber-organized father-in-law had three binders on his office shelf labeled "Helpful Information," "Medical Information," and "Death Binder." If you know, you know what a gift such a sight might be. So when said FIL initiated conversations about his end-of-life planning, my friend tuned him out and thought of other, more lighthearted things – because, sigh, the three helpful binders on the shelves and all. The glory, the relief! When their father passed away, she and her husband slipped into the office and cracked open the three helpful binders on the shelf – only to discover they were empty. Their very organized parent had not made it to the execution part of the death binder project. A big bummer indeed!

So... it's high time to get going on this critical work. The good news is that you don't have to reinvent the wheel or worry you'll forget some necessary tab or document as you assemble everything yourself. There are many death binders, or "In Case of Death" document templates, out there. This one from AARP is pretty good and allows you to fill it out on the line, which is helpful: https://giftplanning.aarp.org/documents/a/aarp-foundation/r1/downloads/record-book.pdf.

A friend told me she made a list of everything essential for her family.

"Get a spreadsheet going of monthly bills, insurance premiums, utilities, lawn care, cleaning service, pest control, income stream, doctors, and regular prescriptions. In other words, how is the household maintained? Who has access to their place?" she suggested. "Getting your arms around the administrative aspects of their lives will help so nothing falls through the cracks! De-clutter, too!"

A super bright, savvy friend in Ponte Vedra Beach runs a Life Management Advisors firm that does this for you with a document they call a Survivor Package. "This is a book of information all about YOU! In it, we will provide every detail of information that your children, POA, or trustee will need to manage your affairs should something happen to you. We will assist you in collecting all the data needed and provide you with a finished copy in a binder and on a USB." I am not kidding when I say this is the best present you could ever give a person you love. The best! Many firms nationwide provide this kind of financial support and senior life management, so I highly encourage you to seek them out and use them!

In the book *How to Care for Aging Parents* by Virginia Morris, she outlines a long checklist of information you will need, and it goes like this:

Names, addresses, and phone numbers of:

- Doctors, dentists, pharmacists, and other medical providers and suppliers

- Lawyers, financial advisers, accountants, and insurance agents

- Banks, investment firms, and other financial institutions

- Clergy members or religious organizations

- Your parent's relatives, close friends, caregivers, and neighbors

The following documents, paperwork and identification:

- Medical history (illness, medications, treatments, allergies, and immunizations)

- Certificates of birth, marriage, divorce/separation, and citizenship

- Military/veterans papers

- Driver's license and passport

- Your parents' will and any changes to the will

- A durable power of attorney

- A living will and power of attorney for health care

- Keys to the house, office, safe deposit box, and post office box, as well as the combination to any safe or lock

- Insurance policies (life, health, disability, homeowners, and auto)

- Social Security, Medicare, and Medicaid numbers and identification cards

- A list of employers, dates of employment, and terms of employment

- Any business contracts or rental agreements

- Deed to the house or rental agreement

- Deeds or titles to real estate, automobiles, boats, and other vehicles

- The location of any valuables, including anything hidden away

- A list of all charge, debit, and banking cards

- Passwords, access codes, PINs

- Any automatic bill-paying or electronic transfer arrangements

- Appraisals of personal property

- Copies of federal and state tax returns from the past three to five years

- Receipts from property taxes and other large recent payments

- Burial and funeral instructions, if any

- Monthly bills (utilities, taxes, mortgage, insurance premiums)

Your parent's assets, including the value of:

- Savings, checking, money market, and retirement accounts.

- Stocks, bonds, and other securities

- Real estate

- Automobiles, boats, and other valuables

- Business ownership and partnership agreements

- Profit-sharing and pension plans

- Trust agreements

- Outstanding loans

- All debts, including mortgages and other loans, credit card balances, outstanding bills, and other liabilities

I also would add contact information for any service provider you use regularly and companies that have helped you manage properties, yourself, or other tools and resources.

Gathering such a massive pile of documents and information takes a lot of work. But listen up. I promise it is the most appreciated and long-remembered pure love gift you can offer your family and friends. It's never too early to start building a death binder that will bring peace, relief, and comfort to your family one day.

Helpful Resources:

Get It Together: Organize Your Records So Your Family Won't Have To, by Melanie Cullen and Shae Irving.

What to Do When I'm Gone: A Mother's Wisdom to Her Daughter.

Everplans.com

Before I Go: The Essential Guide to Creating a Good End of Life Plan, by Jane Duncan Rogers.

Five Wishes

When Breath Becomes Air, by Paul Kalanithi.

Aging with Dignity

The Conversation Project

STEP 2: PEN YOUR OWN OBITUARY AND FUNERAL OBJECTIVES.

THE PROBLEM, IN REAL **talk:**

If you die without communicating critical particulars of your life or how you'd like to be remembered, living loved ones must write an obituary and plan a funeral that may not fit your bill. Not that you'd know this, of course, but others still tottering around on the planet might!

The solution IMHO:

If this is important to you and your family, sit down and hammer out an obituary (or at least some essential dates, accolades, and accomplishments) and some thoughts on your funeral planning, as emotional and challenging as it may be in the moment. Just do it. Then squirrel it away in your death binder or cache of "important documents." Your family will love you forever for this.

One older friend asked me to help plan her funeral – outside, in front of her house, with an open guest list, good music, and a fleet of those "fancy port-a-potties" with actual sinks and good smell-makers galore.

Another friend shared how wonderful it was that her parents had gone to the funeral home, teed up their death management plans, and paid for it. They stipulated they did not want an obituary or a service. I say this is a gift in every way, and more people – all people, IMHO – should be more like my friend's thoughtful, generous, and planful parents.

But the no obituary part was a little gut punch for me, I have to admit. I'm an obituary freak. Obituaries are the last bastion of perfect journalism and local news – they are juicy and exciting and leave you thinking. They tell someone's story of all stories in just a few column inches. They are always a quick but reflective read.

The best part is there is no set standard for an A+, gold-star obituary because, thank God, there's no prescribed form for them anymore. Some are written by the deceased, in letter style to those left behind, and others are short and sweet – funeral information only. Some are about babies and children, which make you wonder and feel sad, then clutch gratitude for the health of the young people you love. Some are like a stale template – they include all the dates, clubs, and accolades and go on for inches and inches without describing much personal detail about the person. Others are so well-written and witty and wonderful that they are plagiarized – by families across the world – repeatedly, as my friend Bonnie Phillips Upright knows well.

One friend said the best thing she ever did was to interview her father about his life before his passing.

"I sat down with my dad a couple of years ago and took notes about what to put in his obituary – I asked him many questions about history, jobs, experiences, and even what the highlights of his life were," she wrote. "It was very sweet and surprising to hear what he wanted – some of which I had no idea, like his exact majors in college and that a highlight he wanted included was a walking tour of England he took a number of years ago."

Whether you're helping a loved one write their obituary or writing your own, an interview is a great place to start.

Just don't let perfectionism get in the way. Remember, there's no one way to skin this cat.

I know people who are obsessed with "doing it right" and worry about what fancy details they want to be included in their obituary, degrees, awards, volunteer leadership, or professional titles and recognitions. They want to ensure it's proper and that the surviving family is listed correctly or in good order. How boring. The best obituaries are ones that perpetuate someone's spirit through authentic storytelling. Besides informing the community of funeral arrangements, which should be the end goal of an obituary — the point is to leave a legacy and to ensure someone (and their good, bad, and/or ugly) is remembered correctly. That and to stay within an affordable column-inch count because truth is, obituaries are freaking expensive. This is a long way of saying, do your family a favor and take a stab at writing your obituary — or make a list with all your important dates and details. That way, whoever's writing or placing your obituary can work with the facts and figure out what they can edit out to, you know, stay within budget.

Whatever your vision for your obituary and funeral might be, the time is now to write down or at least tell someone about your ideas.

Here are a few hints on getting started:

Like most important life tasks, this process begins with quiet reflection time. I might sit down at the beach with a hefty pour of chardonnay and my toes in the sand. Whatever your best-case thinking time looks like, put pen to paper on your major life events, achievements, and people who have been meaningful in your life. This is an excellent time to think about your values and beliefs and how you want to be remembered. This may be hard and make you cry a little! But keep going!

If your ink is running from all your me-tears, go with dates, times, and places. This is easy – and will be very helpful for your loved ones later. Consider graduation and wedding dates, names of your parents, siblings, spouses, and children, degrees you may have achieved and when (and where!), places you worked, and organizations important to you. Maybe some significant accomplishments define you, so write those down, too! Was travel your thing? Reflect on a few trips that influenced your life in some way.

If you want to pen your obituary, consider parameters like writing in the third person and length. Obituaries are sometimes edited for style and are usually priced per column inch, so be careful. When you're done, file it somewhere safe and tell your loved ones where they can find it in a pinch. If you've written your obituary long ago, think to dust it off and update it now and again. Writing your obituary is an empowering way to take control of your narrative and leave a lasting impression on your loved ones. It allows you to preserve your legacy in a way that genuinely reflects who you are and how you want to be remembered.

Perhaps the more challenging exercise is thinking about your funeral arrangements. Let the sobbing commence! You may be a detail person and want to think about all the little things, like songs you'd like to be played at your service, what kind of casket you'd like, or that you prefer to be environmentally sensitive and be cremated, cocooned, or scattered. That's super cool! Write it all down and tell someone about it. Or maybe you want to think in broad strokes, like a burial location or no funeral period. That's great, too! Do whatever brings you peace because that will, in turn, bring your people peace when it comes to knowing how to memorialize you when you're gone.

Helpful Resources:

The Good Death: An Exploration of Dying in America, by Ann Neumann.

Heartfelt Memorial Services: Your Guide for Planning Meaningful Funerals, Celebrations of Life and Times of Remembrance, by Beverly Molander and Dave Savage.

Final Rights: Reclaiming the American Way of Death, by Joshua Slocum and Lisa Carlson.

National Funeral Directors Association (NFDA)

Yours Truly: An Obituary Writer's Guide to Telling Your Story, by James Hagerty.

Dying Well: Peace and Possibilities at the End of Life, by Ira Byock.

Funeral Consumers Alliance

STEP 3: HIRE AN ATTORNEY TO GET LEGIT ABOUT YOUR AFFAIRS.

THE PROBLEM, IN REAL **talk:**

Can we get some order in the court, up in here? If your legal documents, wills, and end-of-life planning paperwork aren't prepared and safely stowed now – long before you think you'll need them – you are opening the door to a major disaster. Those plans for living your best life may be in deep doo-doo!

If this is your current situation, you are not alone.

A 2023 study from Caring.com found that 1 out of 4 Americans without a will never plan on getting one, and more than 40 percent say they plan on waiting until a medical diagnosis. That is the craziest sh** I have ever heard. If this is your thinking, please change the course, stat!

The solution IMHO:

The solution is simple – and highly important. Find a good lawyer specializing in eldercare law or estate planning, and prepare now.

These are the documents you'll want to make sure you have available. According to the National Institute on Aging, this is what you need in your legal bag of goodies as you make your approach to the sunset stroll:

- A will

- A durable power of attorney for finances

- A living trust

- A living will

- A durable power of attorney for healthcare

The National Institute on Aging further recommends putting these important documents in one place and actually telling people you trust where they are located, talking to your loved ones and a doctor about advance care planning, giving permission in advance for a lawyer or doctor to talk to your caregiver as needed, and reviewing your plans regularly.

I like how there's an emphasis on talking to people about your plans in this checklist. That is one of the most fundamental pieces of the plan. Even if you're all squared away legally, other people need to know where to find it all and help execute the plan if you cannot.

Like every other component of a workable grand plan, good legal planning requires preparation, thoughtfulness, and honest, open, and ongoing conversation with the loved ones supporting you along your sunset stroll.

Helpful resources:

American Bar Association

CaringInfo, National Hospice and Palliative Care Organization

The Conversation Project

Eldercare Locator

National Academy of Elder Law Attorneys

National Elder Law Foundation

PREPARE for Your Care

STEP 4: GET YOUR FINANCIAL HOUSE AND PLAN IN ORDER.

THE PROBLEM, IN REAL **talk:**

Financial planning for the senior years is crucial for Americans to ensure a comfortable and secure retirement. As we approach our golden years, we should take specific steps to safeguard our financial well-being. Planning for old age involves considering various factors, including income sources, expenses, investments, and potential healthcare costs.

The problem is, we aren't doing it and later getting ourselves into quite a financial pickle.

A study from the National Council on Aging found that more than 16.5 million Americans over the age of 65 are economically insecure – meaning, they are living at or below 200 percent of the federal poverty level of $45,760 per year for a single person in 2021, according to NCOA.

"These older adults struggle with rising housing and health care bills, inadequate nutrition, lack of access to transportation, diminished savings, and job loss," the study reads. "For older adults above the poverty level, one major adverse life event can change today's realities into tomorrow's troubles."

You got that right.

We forget to discuss and factor in the high – usually way higher than expected – cost of being a senior citizen. The Elder Economic Security Standard Index (Elder Index), a resource developed by the Gerontology Institute at the University of Massachusetts Boston, measures the income older adults need to meet their basic needs and age in place with dignity. It looks at "household size, location, housing tenure, and health status and includes the cost of housing, health care, transportation, food, and miscellaneous essentials." The data is staggering; check it out sometime. I keyed in my city, Duval County, and entered the parameters for a couple in "good" health living in a home with a mortgage. And here are the results for that scenario: this couple needs to have $42,864 a year, which is 88 percent of the national average. Miscellaneous costs for this couple are $499/month, transportation costs are $406/month, housing is $1,373/month, food is $562/month, and health is $782/month for a monthly total of $3,572.

Now, this is a pretend couple with "good" health. Throw in some unexpected medical, health, physical, and mental crises and a dash of significant care needs, and that's when the financial wheels start falling off the bus. That's when you start wishing you had thought about this a little earlier.

A 2023 study from Northwestern Mutual said the "magic number" most Americans have in mind for retirement comfort is $1.27 million. That's some jingle, folks! Yet, at the same time, studies show that many people – 1 in 5, according to a 2023 Axios-Ipsos poll – don't think they'll EVER be able to retire. It's another life pickle that no one's talking about. The Axios-Ipsos poll shows 60 percent of those surveyed aren't talking about it either. An Axios story said the 60 percenters "consider how they might be able to afford retirement often or sometimes, but 41 percent have never discussed saving for retirement with friends, and 57 percent have never spoken about it with a financial planner." Wait, what?

The problem is there's a big, juicy, expensive need on everyone's horizon, yet very few are talking about it with their family, much less the people who can help them prepare for it. This is a huge problem, with devastating consequences.

The solution IMHO:

Get thee to a financial planner as early as humanly possible and start building a strategy now for the long term.

Start by talking to your friends and family about who they use for their financial planning direction. Often, your bank and any investment team you use will have certified financial planners on board to direct you. Use them. They'll ask you for input and personal goals and prepare you with a workable plan.

They can set you up in scenarios that most people need clarification on, and that's how and where to invest your moola. An essential aspect of financial planning for seniors is making sound investment decisions. As we age, investment strategies may shift from aggressive growth-oriented portfolios to more conservative ones focused on income and capital preservation. Diversification is vital to managing risk, and consulting with a financial advisor can help determine the appropriate investment mix for individual circumstances.

Part of the prep work is assessing your current financial situation. This involves calculating your net worth, which includes assets such as savings, investments, property, and retirement accounts, as well as liabilities like debts and mortgages. Having a clear picture of your financial picture makes it easier to understand the starting point and set realistic goals for a blissful senior stroll.

Social Security is a significant income source for many geri-individuals, so it's essential to understand how it works and when to start claiming benefits. Delaying Social Security benefits can lead to higher monthly payments, so it might be beneficial to postpone claiming them until you have reached full retirement age or even beyond. Also, consider other potential income streams, such as pensions or part-time work to supplement retirement funds.

One of my absolute least favorite things to do is to make a budget – but as we age, I think it's pretty critical to the big picture. By analyzing expenses, the older we get, the easier it is to identify areas where we can cut back and ensure retirement income will cover our needs and wants. This is the part where we start playing the "What If?" game regularly. If we aren't planning for unforeseen expenses, such as medical emergencies or home repairs, we could find ourselves in those pickles again – without the funds to pay for them. When budgeting, think of all the things that could go wrong and add that into the budget equation to prevent any financial strain in the future.

Long-term care is the most significant delta in budgeting and planning, as healthcare costs can be substantial. You can talk to your financial advisor about whether or not to buy long-term care insurance to protect assets and provide financial support should you need it. Most people will tell you it's a toss-up and highly dependent on your economic forecast and the timing of its use. The long-term care policies of yore were robust and a smart investment. Today, that's less the case. Many financial planners advise self-insure if you can save the money to do so. Researching and determining whether a long-term care policy suits your needs and budget is essential.

The financial planning conversation should also include elements of the "what do I want my legacy to be" conversation and how you want to support your family and the generations below you. Does your budgeting include leaving money or resources for your children? What's in your will? Does it include helping to cover your grandchildren's educational needs or experiences? Or are you applying all your available funds to retirement on lavish levels? This is up to you, though thinking through the legacy piece is essential. It also involves consultation with your attorney, which surely you have by now. A legal professional can also ensure your assets are aligned via the power of attorney and living will documents, which are essential to designate someone to make financial and medical decisions on your behalf.

Lastly, it's crucial to continue conversations about this and to stay informed about your financial matters. The healthiest family and friend relationships disclose the whole truth and nothing but the truth. Tell your people everything they need to know, especially about financial situations that will involve them one day. There's no need for secrecy or holding back because the more people know, the more they can help.

One friend who had been through the wringer with her parents' financial geri-debacle said she makes sure her children know everything about her financial puzzle.

"After my father's death, I created a document for my family with tons of financial information – monthly withdrawals, loan and credit card information, medical information plus the usual will and lawyer information," she wrote. "I have declared talking about finances is like sex education when the kids are little. Just like everyone has private parts, we all have checking accounts. I don't want my family having to call banks to find out if we banked there."

Your family and trusted friends can also help you stay informed and protect against scams targeting older people. Financial literacy workshops, seminars, and reputable online resources can keep you up-to-date and make informed decisions about your money.

Financial planning for the senior years requires careful thought and planning, attention to detail, and a proactive approach. By using the steps now to assess finances, budget wisely, invest prudently, and plan for healthcare and estate needs, all one-day seniors can better navigate retirement with confidence and security. Seeking advice from financial professionals and discussing plans with family members can provide valuable support.

Helpful Resources:

The Total Money Makeover: A Proven Plan for Financial Fitness, by Dave Ramsey.

Your Money or Your Life: 9 Steps to Transforming Your Relationship with Money and Achieving Financial Independence, by Vicki Robin and Joe Dominguez.

How to Retire Happy, Wild, and Free: Retirement Wisdom That You Won't Get from Your Financial Advisor, by Ernie J. Zelinski.

AARP (American Association of Retired Persons).

Retire Inspired: It's Not an Age, It's a Financial Number, by Chris Hogan

Social Security Administration (SSA)

The Smartest Retirement Book You'll Ever Read, by Daniel R. Solin.

National Institute on Retirement Security (NIRS)

STEP 5: WRITE YOUR OWN PRESCRIPTION FOR HEALTH, HOPE AND HOSPITAL ISSUES AND CONSIDER YOUR MEDICAL THRESHOLDS.

THE PROBLEM, IN REAL **talk:**

There must be clarity about our power over our bodies and minds regarding medical treatment and health care. Too often, people think they must do precisely what the doctor tells them is best – or worse, what their family wants or expects. Of course, taking the recommendation of your doctor and your family isn't the WRONG play when it comes to getting the best health care. But we need to put better thought around what treatment or course of action we believe is right for our unique brand of ourselves, lives, and outcomes, all things considered.

No study I've found defines this issue with tasty statistics or trends. I'm basing this problem on my experiences and those of shared friends or acquaintances.

When my dad was in the hospital on a ventilator, he never got off. We had a pretty good idea that he'd never want aggressive medical treatment, and there were slim chances of bringing him back. That much we knew. Having been through some challenging senior-care scenarios, I now harbor strong opinions about where I want to draw my line with treatment and care. If I'm not contributing actively to this world and I've lived an excellent, full life, I under no circumstances want to have surgery that will keep me around for more of the same. I'll be done. And I'll make sure everyone knows it.

It's all so personal and situational. One person may always seek a very aggressive medical prescription, every time! And that is valiant and super respectable if that person feels they are making a difference in our world and doing life in significant ways and can keep moving forward. Another may feel there's a threshold for their treatment. A financial planner friend says hers is "whether she can wipe her butt," for example.

The problem is we need to articulate our thoughts on this — for ourselves and to others who can help implement them. We need to make sure we are our own best advocates and have the documentation and team in place to support our wishes.

The solution IMHO:

I'm still trying to figure out a perfect solution past giving some thought to your tolerances for health care and treatment. I suppose you can start now by being your medical advocate. That includes soul searching on your health care thresholds, what kind of support you want or need, what your options are, how much it costs, and how friends and family factor into your equation.

A cousin of mine shared this story about her aunt:

"There's a limit on age to having certain surgeries and treatment; decide what that will be and stick to it within reason," she said. "I had a most graceful aunt who said, 'I'm not having physicals after age 75 because I won't be doing anything about what they find, and I'd rather not know.' She died last spring, well into her 90s. She also put herself in a nursing home so her family wouldn't have to make that decision."

Now that's grace! Thinking and talking about medical thresholds is a generous first step for your family. The second step is ensuring all your medical paperwork is in order. Know what you need to confirm your wishes are respected and make them official long before you have to make that surprise visit to the hospital. That paperwork should include any medical directives, living wills, health care powers of attorney, do-not-resuscitate orders, and the like. Again, make sure you've talked to "your person(s)" about any role they play in this paperwork, and tell people where to find the documents in case you're not around.

After a challenging situation with her parents, a friend said she and her husband made sure their medical paperwork was current and ready to execute.

"We will be certain that our health care powers of attorney, durable powers of attorney, living wills, and do-not-resuscitate orders are up-to-date and are printed on the right color paper – yes, really. Florida, where my parents live, requires the DNR be on yellow paper," she wrote. "EMTs, emergency rooms, and other health care facilities will disregard it if it's on white paper. Also, my father's Power of Attorney documents and living will, which were done and executed in 2002, had to be updated before anyone would accept them. We were lucky that he was lucid enough the day my parents' lawyer went to his bedside to update them. Had he not been 'of right mind,' we would have had to go through a long and costly guardianship process before we could, say, engage his long-term care policy."

With proper documentation secured, you might also consider some medical and caregiving services available to elderly patients. If you want to manage your care and can afford to do so, consider working with a senior care management firm that can oversee your health and care needs. Though expensive, geriatric care managers (some on staff at hospitals and senior living centers) can take the pressure off a challenging caregiving situation, especially for your family or "person."

Another service to consider straight away is hospice care. Hospice has such a bad rap. You say hospice care, and people immediately think of buzzards circling or a crypt keeper lurking in the shadows. That is not accurate whatsoever. Hospice is life-giving care, and most times, depending on the provider, it is free. As long as you are in some form of decline with a terminal condition and your doctor signs off on it, you can utilize the hospice system's perks. That includes weekly visits from a nurse, assistance with bathing and grooming, home assistance, medications, medical devices, and even adult diapers – all free to you. Should you need or want it, you can also receive hospice care in a hospice facility, where trained staff are available 24-7. Hospice relationships are evaluated every six months and can continue for years, so make sure it's on your radar for consideration.

Another friend shared this:

"Inquire about palliative care offered through hospice," she wrote. "As patient and family become overwhelmed by endless medical appointments and treatment, one needs a patient-centered program as offered through palliative care and traditional hospice."

Noted. I cannot say enough good things about hospice care and wish more people would consider it earlier in their healthcare and aging journey.

The best thing we can do for ourselves is to stay informed about all the things – about our medical conditions, medications, and treatment options. I think this can be an empowering process for making well-informed health decisions. Add to this keeping good records of your medical history and telling people where they can access them!

Per the uzshe in grand planning, communication is critical when advocating for your health. Communicate clearly with your healthcare providers, yes, but keep your family and friends in the loop regarding how you want to be provided care. During those talks, you can address issues like second opinions and medications and their impacts on others. Make sure you share the important stuff, like how you want your pain managed or how much is too much care from your perspective.

The more people you inform, the better advocate for yourself you are being.

And, of course, one of the best things you can do is prioritize preventative care – get vaccinated and screened when you're told to, have regular check-ups, and make healthy choices to catch problems early.

Being your best medical advocate and taking an active role in your healthcare decisions – and most importantly, TALKING ABOUT IT – fosters a collaborative relationship with healthcare providers and families that can make hard choices more manageable. By staying informed and communicating openly, we can enhance our quality of life and navigate sunset strolls with confidence and dignity.

Helpful Resources:

Being Mortal: Medicine and What Matters in the End, by Atul Gawande.

Advance Care Planning (ACP) Decisions

The Conversation Project

Prepare for Your Care website

National Institute on Aging (NIA)

STEP 6: EDUCATE YOURSELF ON THE COST, SCOPE AND REALITY OF THE GERI-LIFE YOU ENVISION – PARTICULARLY YOUR RESIDENCE.

THE PROBLEM, IN REAL **talk:**

Many older adults are reluctant to get honest about the expense, practicality, and manageability of their vision for golden-year greatness – especially regarding where they will live. Whether planning to age in place, move to a retirement community, or live with a loved one, we aren't always considering the realities of it all. When we're not educated on the options, we make costly mistakes that can negatively impact our senior experience and family relationships. When we choose not to think about it until crisis time – we are SCREWED.

Compounding the screwed-ness is this reality: the aging population in the United States is growing exponentially, and there is an absence of housing.

According to the U.S. Department of Housing and Urban Development: "The Harvard Joint Center for Housing Studies (JCHS) projects that the number of U.S. adults aged 65 and older will grow from 48 to 79 million over the next two decades. By 2035, JCHS expects that 50 million households — approximately 1 out of every 3 in the United States — will be headed by someone age 65 or older, and the number of people aged 80 and older will double to 24 million. The nation's existing housing stock — in terms of options, affordability, and accessibility — is ill-suited to meet the housing needs of an increasingly older population that overwhelmingly wishes to age in place."

A recent study from the National Council on Aging and the Leading Age LTSS Center at the University of Massachusetts Boston shows 60 percent of older adults – that's 24 million households – do not have the funds to pay for in-home, long-term care, which is the most significant factor determining whether aging in place is even an option. According to research, most of us want to age in place – but haven't made financial plans for it. The 2021 AARP Home and Community Preferences Survey sheds some light on how seniors are envisioning their living arrangements, according to AARP:

- Most adults say they don't want to move.

- Two-thirds of those surveyed said they want a combination of help from family and paid professionals in their homes.

- 18 percent expect to relocate to a different residence in their community.

- 29 percent think they will go to a different community.

- 44 percent want to live in a multigenerational neighborhood.

- 32 percent want an active 55+ community.

- 32 percent prefer a continuing care community.

- 69 percent would consider sharing their home with a relative or friend as they age.

- 4 percent have an accessory dwelling unit (ADU) on their property, and 26 percent would consider having one.

And what about assisted living, nursing home, or continuing care options? There's a lot to consider when it comes to senior residential options. And no option is cheap. When we aren't thinking about the scope and cost of our senior living dreams, it's like taking a big bag of moola marked "golden year dough," cutting a hole in the bottom, and watching in horror as the entire bag empties.

You're in luck if the care you need is for something medical — skilled nursing home or facility care is usually covered to some degree by Medicare, which is a great relief for a medically-induced, short-term situation. But that hole in the bottom of the bag gets much bigger if you or your loved one needs help with butt-wiping or getting to the kitchen without falling or with some chronic disorder that inhibits but is not life-threatening. The bottom about falls out of the bag entirely if that non-skilled nursing care is needed 24 hours a day. If you estimate care costs of $25 an hour, 24 hours a day, seven days a week, that's a whopping $600 a day, $4,200 a week, and $218,400 a year.

If you say something like, "It's only temporary; this couldn't possibly last forever," chances are you are very, very wrong. See, the thing about planning care is that you just. Don't. Know. It could be six weeks, or it could be six years.

Elder living needs are fluid and unpredictable and require us to play the "What If?" and "Ask Yourself Honestly" games (see soft steps) long before we make the decision to move or renovate or put our name on "the list" at some continuing care community. The problem is we need to be.

The solution IMHO:

Good news! Plenty of resources and options exist for us to peruse as we make our way toward the golden years. And doing even the slightest bit of research on it – or having the tiniest few honest conversations about it – will help us make intelligent decisions for our unique situations.

Let's talk about the options most people consider for senior living arrangements. What's good for you or your loved one depends on myriad factors, including financial wherewithal, health, mobility, family dynamics, and resource needs. Being honest about what you like, what you need, and what you can afford should be the lens through which you evaluate your plans.

As we discussed earlier, the aging-in-place model is the most prevalent thought for elder living. If a mortgage is paid off and a family is nearby to offer free assistance, aging-in-place can be a financially responsible choice. This option allows for maximum independence and familiarity.

But it can also get expensive quickly when considering the cost of in-home caregiving, accommodation renovations, and maintenance. The costs associated with aging in place include one-time home modifications for accessibility, such as installing grab bars or ramps, ongoing utility expenses, property taxes, home maintenance, and healthcare services. It can get pricey, trust me!

Prepping your home for senior living involves expensive additions, including:

- Accessibility upgrades such as widening doorways, installing ramps, and eliminating barriers between rooms

- Bathroom modifications for safe and accessible use

- Kitchen adaptations, including lower countertops and modified faucets, shelving, and storage that make daily tasks easier

- Lighting and flooring that make getting around the house clearer and less inhibited, especially for future wheelchair or walker use

- Technology integration for motion sensor lighting and convenient voice-activated controls

- Home security to keep you and your valuables safe and connected to help should you need it

- Heating, cooling, and insulation to help reduce energy costs

- Emergency communication systems that can get emergency help to you quickly

- General repairs and upkeep to ensure your home is salable and holds its value

Renovating a home for age-in-place living can be a considerable expense. Still, if you invest in these improvements, you can maintain their independence, stay in familiar surroundings, and enjoy a safer and more comfortable living environment as you age. So that's positive.

However, the big negative with that aging-in-place plan is that you can often be unprepared – financially and socially – to deal with unexpected emergencies. Sadly, this is the way it goes for many families. When asked what she'd do differently from her parents' caregiving experience, one friend suggested she would never wait until it was too late to plan for other living arrangements.

"We will not wait too long to leave our two-story home and move into a place where we can build a group of friends and support system before we need it, and where our daughter can be certain we will be cared for as we age," she wrote. "I begged my parents for years to get out of that house. They'd visit retirement communities and eat the free lunch but not make a move. Then, my dad had a stroke, and everyone panicked. We were super lucky to find a place for them to go, let alone a place they love, which they do. The chance they would have had to take something they DIDN'T love was high at that point because they had to go somewhere. I credit the Holy Spirit. There's no other explanation."

The lesson here is to know your options when it comes to housing arrangements. Luckily, there are lots of options out there. One of the most popular alternatives for aging-in-place is moving to a continuing care retirement community or CCRC. This is my first choice. My grandmothers lived in a place like this, and it was awesome. You pay to live in a home there independently and then can progress through other arrangements as your health needs dictate. These are expensive, though, so start saving your pennies now.

Another option is an independent living community – a retirement community or an active adult communities. These places look pretty attractive if you ask me. The perks I see are a reduction in maintenance costs and responsibilities, opportunities to socialize and stay active, and a chance to downsize and start fresh in an attractive place. This is up there on my list. It's not a cheap option, either. Let's get that out of the way now: none of these options is inexpensive. That's why we have a financial plan for it all now! The cost of choosing independent living comes in monthly rent, entry fees, and annual fees – so start saving now!

If you think, or find, that you need a bit of care assistance – and paying for in-home care or depending on a friend or family member is out of the question – then an assisted living facility is something to consider. They cater to seniors who need help with daily activities like bathing, dressing, and medication management but still have independence. Assisted living fees cover everything from housing, meals, housekeeping, personal care, activities, and transportation to places like the grocery store or appointments. This varies from place to place, and some spaces are covered by Medicaid, depending on your financial situation.

It's the same story with nursing homes, where you might go when your medical and care needs are more significant. Sometimes called skilled nursing facilities, these places provide care 24-7. Nursing homes can be expensive because residents receive such skilled, around-the-clock care. And costs increase the more care and monitoring, caregiving and attention you need.

The most inexpensive financially – but riskiest from a relationship perspective – is multigenerational living, a common practice in many countries outside the United States. According to 2019 "Pop Facts" statistics from the United Nations, "living with a child or with extended family members was the most common living arrangements among older persons in Africa, Asia and Latin America and the Caribbean, whereas in Europe, Northern America, Australia, and New Zealand, living with a spouse only was the most common arrangement, followed by living alone." A 2020 Pew Research Center study showed "in the U.S., 27% of adults ages 60 and older live alone, compared with 16% of adults in the 130 countries and territories studied. In many countries in the Asia-Pacific, sub-Saharan Africa, and the Middle East-North Africa regions – such as Afghanistan, Mali, and Algeria – fewer than 5% of seniors live alone."

This option can positively impact a family but can also wear thin on adult children's lifestyle and privacy. It's very personal and unique to everyone's individual situation. This only works if everyone's expectations align and conversations occur early on. Conversation is the key, once again!

When considering living options, we should be factoring in current financial resources, potential healthcare needs, personal preferences, and the level of social engagement we desire. Sound financial planning and understanding of resources can help our senior selves and our families make informed decisions about the most suitable living arrangements for the Golden Years.

Helpful resources:

Eldercare Locator

Centers for Medicare & Medicaid Services

USAging

Department of Housing and Urban Development

Low-Income Home Energy Assistance Program

National Resource Center on Supportive Housing and Home Modifications

STEP 7: MINIMIZE THE HELL OUT OF YOURSELF AND YOUR STUFF.

THE PROBLEM, IN REAL **talk:**

All the stuff we accumulate during our lifetime – the clothes, the serving pieces, the plates, the Hummel figurine collection, second homes, brown furniture, and decades-old towels and linens – doesn't just magically disappear when we die or stroke out or get rushed to a rehabilitation or assisted living center after a freak crisis. It sits there, smirking at our loved ones until they muster the blind courage to just freaking purge it once and for all.

Real talk newsflash: your people do not want, need, or covet your stuff. While there may be a few things in your collection someone will admire or enjoy – or, at best, use to improve their life experience somehow – most of it will go to Goodwill or the trash pile or become someone's big dusty find at an estate or garage sale. Don't kid yourself that the proceeds from this sale will be a financial windfall for anyone involved. Your loved ones will probably pay people to make it gone. Getting rid of all your stuff will take an emotional toll on your people because it hurts to the core to see you and your story disappear.

It also Isn't a quick, simple, or easy task. It's trauma by every measure. It's physically and emotionally exhausting. And your people will have to take personal days – multiple days they might have spent on a much-needed vacation time, appointments, or family respite – to get this big, yucky job done.

"Do not ever imagine that anyone will wish—or be able—to schedule time off to take care of what you didn't bother to take care of yourself. No matter how much they love you, don't leave this burden to them," said Margareta Magnusson in her bestselling book, *The Gentle Art of Swedish Death Cleaning: How to Make Your Loved Ones' Lives Easier and Your Own Life More Pleasant.*

When your loved ones toss your prized hoarded items to the curb, it's like losing you all over again. It's painful and will take your people a long time to heal from the clean-up. Hella. Long. Time.

Another major problem with clutter and stuff is that multiple studies show it causes depression and tripping hazards for older adults. A January 2019 headline in the New York Times called it "unbearable heaviness," with the subhead: "A cluttered home can be a stressful home." Stuff is terrible for our health!

The other big prize you need to purge is you – rather, that self-seeking side of you that hasn't learned how to exit stage left and let the other people in your life slide into the spotlight. This is your time to teach, love, and encourage from a front-row seat. Getting older is a time of lessening. This is the time to reflect, emphasize the softer side of life, and share all the glorious wisdom and experience you've gained over the years. You have some special strengths to share!

But refusing to fade into the background, or worse, living whole hog in the spotlight with zero awareness of your audience impact, will build resentment. Promise. Your biggest fans may even walk out on you or give you a bad review. Who the heck wants that? You need those people! And they need the life lessons you've been tucking away for the right time. And the right time is now.

The solution IMHO:

Here's the good news. Like many of the solutions in this book, the only hard work required of you is to consider the reality of it. Just think about it for a minute. Reflect on your stuff and what you think will happen to it. Take account of all your worldly possessions and consider how they bring you joy – or not.

A more humble, less possessive approach will then inform your actions. It may lead you to conversations with your children, grandchildren, or younger friends about what items of yours they admire, might enjoy, or might be itching to use in their lives. No matter what stuff-plan these dialogues yield, you must not take any of it personally. Your people may not want one more thing to care for in your life. They may love you but not share your taste in anything! They also may be trying to purge and pare down. Your shine may have worn off your stuff, and it's simply not attractive to anyone. It's all OK. This is not about you – or your loved one. It's just...Stuff. And you don't need very much of it.

Now that you've understood what's important to whom, it's time to consider a purge of epic proportions. Go through all the drawers, closets, and shelves and make a mental or actual pile of anything you don't use or like. If you have the energy, flog it all out onto the driveway and sell it for bargain-hunter prices. If not, hire an estate sale company or auction house to assess your collection of well loved pieces. Let them sell it to the people they think will be interested. But never, under any circumstances, expect a windfall, a small fortune, or your nest egg for senior living greatness to result. Your stuff has very little value in the big scheme of things. Let that expectation settle in, and be ready for it. No tears, please.

Got a storage unit full of crap you haven't seen in 10 years? Lord have mercy; that needs to go right this minute! Storage facility companies are notorious for jacking up monthly rental fees every time it rains, so the $75 a month you paid last year is now costing you and your estate double or triple that figure. Quickly think if there's anything in that unit that is important or brings happiness to your life. Then, ask your people if they need or want anything in there. If the answer is no, thank you, then call a nonprofit organization or a junk removal company to meet you at that storage unit and make it all disappear. Then don't ever think about it again. Life is too short to be weighed down by stuff you don't use, like, or need.

Here are a few other anti-stuff, pro-purge words to live by:

- Start small and set goals, beginning with one area at a time. Set achievable goals so you don't feel overwhelmed.

- Sort your stuff into "keep, donate, sell, or recycle" piles This makes the pitch ten billion times more manageable and liberating.

- Be like my brother-in-law, Tom, and abide by the one-year rule: toss it if you last used the item a year ago. Set free the stuff that no longer serves a purpose in your life.

- Apply the same decluttering principles to your interweb junk – delete, unsubscribe, and remove.

- Set your sentimental sh** a sail. Take pictures of the things that may be special but serve no purpose and send them to your family and friends.

- Also, a BIL Tom rule: follow the "one-in, one-out" rule. Hold yourself accountable for removing an item of equal value when you bring something new into your home.

- Donate or sell your unnecessary, unwanted items so someone else can benefit from them.

Keep cleaning and continue purging. When cleaning out, you will never reach "the bottom" of your stuff collection. Stay at it, and don't be overrun by the stuff again.

This freedom and peace of mind from simplifying physical possessions are well worth the time and energy – promise. Do these things, and you'll be ready for your next move, whatever that looks like. You will be well prepared to sell your big house and move into something more manageable. You can snap your fingers and, in an instant, be packed and ready to take up residence at your child's home, in a senior living arrangement, or in an environment that best supports your physical, emotional, and mental needs. You will be ready now.

You will also be mentally prepared to live a purged, pared-back, perfectly pleasant life.

"As energy becomes a precious and limited resource, simplifying is a survival skill. I've learned to beware of 'the disease of one more thing' – We try to let go of the unimportant and stick with what gives us the most meaning, comfort, and joy. This is a fine time to think about what you hold dear and make sure you are spending your precious life doing it," said Katy Butler in her book *The Art of Dying Well: A Practical Guide to a Good End of Life*. "Moving to a smaller house, reducing the size of a lawn and the number of mutual fund accounts, putting bills on auto-pay, and decluttering possessions can help you stay independent longer. Keep the tasks of daily life manageable as energy and mental clarity wane. You can also apply the principle of simplification to the doctors you see, the health screenings you permit, and the pills you take."

A stuff reduction – in thought or action – also will help pare back that inflated sense of self you might still be dragging around. You'll feel more compelled to simplify on that front, too. Remember, you are right now rocking your second half of life. This is when we should look for opportunities to share, teach, inspire, and impart. Are there younger people who might benefit from the strengths you honed during the first half of your life? Are there lessons you've learned that can sustain those in another generation? Is there a philosophy or moral code you've found to be helpful? Seek out and connect to an audience for the messaging only you can put into the world.

"The service that the whole world needs from the elders is not the service of hours spent and time put in and documents finished, and machines fixed. There are untold numbers of people who can do all of those things. No, the service of elders is not a service of labor; it is a service of enlightenment, wisdom, and discernment of spirits," said Joan Chittister in her book *The Gift of Years*. "Only the carriers of generations past can give us those things because wisdom is what lasts after an experience ends. We cannot expect wisdom as a wholesale item of the young, then, because they simply have not lived long enough or through enough to have been able to amass much of it."

Volunteering, focusing on community service, helping others less fortunate than you, and looking for ways to make a difference are your most effective de-selfers. Use them as much as you can! Make friends with younger people and celebrate, understand, and influence their hard work. Become more aware of what's essential to your loved ones and seek ways to support them. Soon, that old bag of self will be a super light superhero cape that doesn't take up any room on the stage and always saves the day. Plus, it's an ordinary course of human existence. Embrace it!

Here are a few ways to get your arms around this important new normal and let your ego fade into the sunset:

- Be mindful and meditate.

- Practice gratitude.

- Sharpen your empathy.

- Serve others and engage in acts of kindness and service.

- Practice detachment from the physical things that define you.

- Remember that everything is impermanent.

- Be a study of philosophy and spiritual concepts.

- Engage in activities that are not driven by personal gain.

That should seal the deal!

"The existence of the second curve is great news for all of us. First, we now have an explanation for the typical drop-off in abilities in one's forties or fifties. In other words, if you are my age or older, it isn't just you. Second, there is a second wave to ride to success that favors people who are older. Third, by most estimations, what you get in this second wave is more valuable (if less lucrative and prestigious) than what you get in the first. After all, as the saying goes, 'knowledge is knowing that a tomato is a fruit; wisdom is knowing not to put it in a fruit salad,'" said Arthur C. Brooks, in his book *From Strength to Strength: Finding Success, Happiness and Deep Purpose in the Second Half of Life.*

This work is essential. That's why it's high up on the Grand Plans list. Don't leave your loved ones with a house full of dusty trinkets, furnishings, and a first-class assemblage of BS. Don't let your earthly legacy be one of me, me, me. Reducing, minimizing, lessening, becoming "more free" – it's the first rule of this Grand Planning game.

Helpful resources

The Gentle Art of Swedish Death Cleaning: How to Free Yourself and Your Family from a Lifetime of Clutter by Margaretta Magnusson

Other books on purging your stuff:

The Life-Changing Magic of Tidying Up: The Japanese Art of Decluttering and Organizing by Marie Kondo

Let it Go: Downsizing Your Way to a Richer, Happier Life by Peter Walsh

Keep the Memories, Lose the Stuff: Declutter, Downsize and Move Forward with Your Life by Matt Paxton with Jordan Michael Smith

The Joy of Less: A Minimalist Guide to Declutter Organize and Simplify by Francine Jay

A few books on minimizing self in the second half of life:

The Gift of Years: Growing Older Gracefully by Joan Chittister

From Strength to Strength: Finding Success, Happiness and Deep Purpose in the Second Half of Life by Arthur C. Brooks

Falling Upward: A Spirituality for the Two Halves of Life by Fr. Richard Rohr

The Art of Dying Well: A Practical Guide to a Good End of Life by Katy Butler

Step 8: Consider pet acquisitions carefully.

THE PROBLEM, IN REAL **talk:**

Pets complicate the management of our Golden Year glory, yet they are scientifically shown to improve the experience. It's a real co-nundrum. While there's no doubt pets are an important part of the algebra, we aren't factoring in the big variable: what happens when we die or can't care for them anymore? We aren't talking about how this situation impacts others in our sphere. No bones about it, folks; we are keeping a tight leash on the conversations that matter. And that's a rough situation.

One elderly couple I befriended had a huge dog in their house that caused many problems. There were fundamental issues like taking the dog to the vet or purchasing supplies when neither could drive. Then there were financial issues like paying for the dog's vet care or supplies when every penny went to 24-7 home health care. Then there was the issue of options. Having a dog meant they didn't have any if they want-ed to go to an assisted living center, hire the nice caregiver allergic to dogs, or even lower the medical bed because...big dogs jump on things and mess sh** up when they're not getting the attention and exercise they need.

Another friend recalled how her father-in-law adopted a puppy in his 80s despite everyone telling him what a bad idea that was given his situation. When reality hit, and he had to leave the house for a bit, he tied the dog up in the front yard – until some kind neighbor stepped in to assist.

On the news, there's a recurring story about some elderly hoarder who gets rushed to the hospital – and dies, maybe – and leaves behind a houseful of pets and pet yuck. Pets that someone ELSE must manage. It happens all the time.

Where is the reality check? Where's the real talk? A non-existent conversation about the existence and future of pets is a problem.

The solution IMHO:

Don't worry. I won't advocate for some "no dogs allowed" policy for seniors. Nor will I encourage you to run to the pet adoption center and grab a couple of cats for your stable. My job today is to encourage you – once again – to find the humility, self-awareness, and grace to talk to your people about it. My thesis here is to get everyone on the same page, even when it comes to your furry friends.

Pets are a big part of our lives – let's start with that fact. A University of Michigan National Poll on Healthy Aging showed that 55 percent of 2,000 U.S. adults aged 50-80 owned at least one pet. Other studies show senior pet ownership is about 50 percent for Americans over 50. That seems about right. And we spend significant funds on them, too. The latest figures (2021) from the APPA (American Pet Products Association) suggest that Americans spend *more than $123.6 billion* on their pets. So, about half of all elderly adults are investing a chunk of change each year on their furry friends.

And the investment is paying off. A 2019 *TIME* magazine piece said, "Nearly 90% of older pet owners said their animals helped them enjoy life and feel loved; roughly 80% said their pets reduced stress; and almost three-quarters said their furry friends provided a sense of purpose, according to the poll. In addition, 64% of pet owners — and 78% of dog owners — said their pets helped them stay physically active. Sixty percent also said their pets helped them cope with physical and emotional health issues."

But the article also described the drawbacks, which is the crux of the problem here.

"People did report a few drawbacks to pet ownership, including difficulty traveling or leaving the house (54%) and financial strains (18%). Six percent of pet owners said they'd fallen or injured themselves due to having a pet — consistent with a recent study finding rising fractures among elderly dog owners. Fifteen percent of pet owners, including 26% who said they were in fair or poor health, said their pet's health took precedence over their own."

A while back, a Grand Plans friend was lamenting their elderly and infirm parents' decision to home a new dog and how seemingly short-sighted that choice had been. The dog's destiny was to be on some unsuspecting but charitable human's dole, like it or not. Pets can be a real anchor point! And they can live a long, long time. On the flip side, it's a fact that pets make humans' quality of life so much better. They help emotionally, intellectually, and spiritually; some pets are even trained to provide service or render aid. It's a challenging situation. At the very least, getting a pet later in life necessitates a frank conversation with the people caring for you, me, and us.

Helpful Resources:

American Society for the Prevention of Cruelty to Animals (ASPCA)

AARP: Pets and Livable Communities

Pets for the Elderly Foundation

Local animal shelters and rescue organizations: These groups often have programs specifically designed for senior adopters and can provide guidance on choosing a pet that matches the owner's lifestyle, offer support in pet selection, and provide information about low-cost veterinary services.

Step 9: Relinquish the keys and be ready – eager even! – to be a passenger.

THE PROBLEM, IN REAL **talk:**

A friend was recounting a story to me about the grocery store parking lot totaling of her Buick Lacrosse – "white, with Florida tags," the voice on the loudspeaker described. She left her cart and exited the store to find "a sweet little ole lady had hit the gas instead of the brakes while attempting to park." She said the impact pushed her car halfway out of the parking space, rendering it a total loss.

"The gal couldn't understand what happened, and she was so sorry – sound familiar?" my friend texted.

The older woman's son arrived shortly after, "absolutely horrified."

"He has been trying to get her to stop driving for months," she wrote. "I told him this was his opportunity to divest her of the car keys permanently. This accident probably totaled my car. Next time, it could be injury or death of a person. He said he'd have the conversation with her that day."

And that there is the long and short of the problem.

Many older adults aren't "giving up the keys" or "retiring from driving" until a family argument, traffic incident, or medical emergency ensues, and that kind of obstinance is dangerous for everyone – and it's getting worse with the increase of elderly adults on the road.

In *Honest Aging: An Insider's Guide to the Second Half of Life* by Rosanne M. Leipzig, MD Ph. D, she said drivers 85 and older have the highest rates of fatal accidents per mile driven, with the rate for drivers 80-84 years old is similar to that of teenagers.

According to a 2022 study from the National Safety Council, the number of motor vehicle deaths involving drivers and other road users aged 65 and older increased by 15 percent from 7,902 in 2020 to 9,102 in 2021. The study showed that the number of deaths increased by 34 percent in the past decade. At the same time, the population of older adults in the United States grew 29 percent, resulting in a death rate per 100,000 population increase of 2.5 percent. The study noted that these fatality trends are based on mortality data collected by the Centers for Disease Control and Prevention.

Based on this CDC data, in 2021, older adult motor-vehicle deaths included:

- 486 non-traffic deaths

- 1,952 vehicle occupant traffic deaths

- 609 motorcyclist traffic deaths

- 1,645 pedestrian traffic deaths

- 180 bicyclist traffic deaths

- And 4,230 other or unspecified traffic deaths

It's a problem, folks. And yes, it's a problem that creates other problems. Older adults who can no longer drive worry their independence is compromised without access to a car. They are right. And many seniors – 80 percent, according to a 2018 study from the National Aging and Disability Transportation Center – say they can't do what they want to do anymore because of a transportation shortage. This also is true.

But with the advent of better transportation technology (read cool apps like Uber, Lyft, and even Go-Go Grandparent) and some discernment on where we live and our proximity to public transportation or walkable destinations, "giving the keys up" doesn't have to be the final act that sends us into a tailspin of epic proportions.

The solution IMHO:

I'm putting all my hope in driverless car technology as I approach Golden Years. That would solve everything when it's time for me to stop driving.

I was going to say when it was time to "take my keys away," but that's a horrible phrase, and too many of us are using it. Driving is a privilege; yes, it stinks when someone suggests that the risks outweigh the privilege. Still, it's more about being released from the responsibility than having your keys snatched.

I look forward to it, take my damn keys now, LOL. I know it feels like your independence is wrecked. Still, if you're expecting it and anticipating this milestone with some excitement around finally being the passenger, it feels less like taking and more like, heck yeah, I have arrived!

There's too much technology out there now to be afraid of being de-independenced on our sunset stroll between the Ubers and the driverless cars and the drones that will airlift us places. One more thing to put on our What to Expect When You're Expecting to be Old list: You will have to stop driving one day, which will be no big deal. If that thought IS a big deal, however, it's time to consider moving to a place that offers walk- or scoot-ability to all the places you need to access for life's happiness.

Some creative people have devised a plan for setting themselves straight ahead of time by signing contracts when everything is still a little more straightforward. AAA has a Drivers Planning Agreement on the interwebs with a quick search. It's a simple contract that includes easy-to-understand tenets of safe driving standards and contingencies, planning for the inevitable time we take our hands off the steering wheel and let someone else drive. Here are a few of them:

- "I realize that the natural aging process may, at some point in the future, affect my ability to drive safely. By taking the time now to work closely with my family, I can develop a plan to ensure my safety and the safety of others while also maintaining my mobility and independence. The most important thing my family can do is to help me explore all of my options to keep me driving or mobile. If concerned about my driving abilities, help me access the appropriate resources or services that can potentially mitigate these concerns so that I may safely drive. Examples include, but are not limited to:"

- Help me find an occupational therapist who is trained to address the problems that put me at risk behind the wheel and equipped to develop an individualized plan to use moving forward.

- Ensure that I am able to visit my primary care physician or local pharmacist to review how medications I take may affect my driving.

- Assist me in accessing an eye doctor or vision care specialist who can address my needs.

- Help me determine how I can appropriately self-regulate when and where I drive so that I maintain maximum comfort and safety behind the wheel; and

- Encourage me to take a driver-improvement course to refresh my skills and learn new techniques for adapting to my changing needs as an aging driver.

The great discussion points of this document go on a bit, and it's all EX-CELLENT brain fodder for all of us as our thinking gets a little cloudier and we become defiant about someone taking away our autonomy.

The Alzheimer's Association also warehouses a similar driver's contract on its website. It also suggests bringing in other trusted friends and family members to the conversation and professionals who can underscore the message: "Solicit the support of others. Ask your physician to advise the person not to drive. Involving your physician in a family conference on driving may be more effective than persuading the person not to drive alone. Ask the physician to write a letter or prescription stating that the person with dementia must not drive. You can then use the document to remind your family members what's been decided. Ask a respected family authority figure or your attorney to reinforce the message about not driving. When the person is still in the early stage of dementia, ask them to sign a driving contract that permits you to help them stop driving when the time comes."

You may be willing to self-regulate or help a senior friend figure it out. According to AARP, there are a few "red flags" to be on the lookout for when giving up the keys is the best strategy:

- Medical issues

- Driving too slow or too fast consistently

- Getting lost on familiar roads

- Having recent car accidents or near misses

- Having trouble parking or turning left

- Receiving tickets for moving violations

- Running red lights or stop signs

- Showing up with new dents or scratches on the car

- Using lanes improperly

At the end of the day, know you have options if you aren't able to drive anymore. In *Honest Aging: An Insider's Guide to the Second Half of Life*, Leipzig suggests the following transportation alternatives to driving: walking; train or subway; bus; taxi or ride-sharing services; family and friends; community transportation services; hospital shuttles; medi-car, volunteer drivers; or private for-profit senior care services.

Retirement from driving does not mean you've been put out to pasture or are stuck at home for the rest of your life. It just means more Grand Planning 101: expect and accept this every-human condition; communicate about it; trust your people on acceptable ways to handle it; research and learn how to use tools or resources that will improve it; and make provisions and line items on how you'll plan for it. In the case of driver retirement, you'll want always to remember these realities: you can't drive forever; you must consider proximity to sources of transportation – biking, walking, or public resources – when you make plans for your senior housing; technology to help you exists if you will dedicate your mind to learning and using it; and all these considerations have financial implications that you'll need to make workable grand plans far in advance.

Giving up on driving is another rite of passage toward self-lessening and letting go. We must get comfortable with the fact we can't do life the same way we could in our younger years, and that is OK. Like, super OK. It's normal. We must stop thinking there's a way to change our human destiny. We must figure out ways to plan for it, accept it, and move on.

Helpful resources:

AAA Driving Contract

Alzheimer's Association's Driving Contract

Honest Aging: An Insider's Guide to the Second Half of Life by Rosanne M. Leipzig MD PhD

Intermission, A Grand Pause

B EFORE WE GET TO the soft steps, the last 11 on my list, I want to ensure you know I am not pulling all these suggestions out of my 51-year-old empty-nester a**. There's some important historical and philosophical context here that we should get out of the way first. Humor me, please, with a quick overview of how this Grand Plan thinking evolved and aligns with what smarter, more experienced people throughout history have been putting into the universe.

These 20 steps to a grand plan for geri-living excellence are nothing new. The ingredients for a full and successful third act have been floating around for centuries. These themes have been published in books – including THE book – heck, on tablets and painted on cave walls. Intelligent people have been on this for a long, long time.

One of the most common urgings of writers, philosophers, and faith leaders is the idea of minimizing. It is on every smart writer's list of geri-musts. Take Margareta Magnusson's world-famous book *The Gentle Art of Swedish Death Cleaning: How to Free Yourself and Your Family from a Lifetime of Clutter*. That is the thesis of her everything – stuff and obsession with self is dreadfully unimportant and weighty as we age. So best to clear it all out – the crap we don't use, the stuff we don't want, and especially the image of ourselves as defined by it all.

"Life will become more pleasant and comfortable if we get rid of some of the abundance," Magnusson says in the book, and that's a tremendous understatement. Paring back is the single most loving act we can affect for our children and family.

In Katy Butler's bestselling book *The Art of Dying Well: A Practical Guide to a Good End of Life*, she shares a similar bulleted list for preparing for the first stages of getting older. This book is required reading if you're into this sort of subject matter, as is her other bestseller *Knocking on Heaven's Door*. Here are a few excerpts from Butler's "ways to prepare" list at the end of Chapter 2, which is the part about early-on, easy stuff – when you're aging but not at the geri-emergency stage. See any parallels?

- "Start with what requires the most from you and the least from medicine. Get half an hour or more of vigorous, pleasurable exercise every day;"

- "Get to know neighbors, cultivate friendships with younger people, help friends who are sick, and find ways to mentor and to give;"

- "Pick a medical advocate and talk openly about your fears and wishes;"

- "Prepare not only for death but for dementia and disability. Fill out forms to allow a trusted friend or spouse to be your 'authorized representative' with Medicare, access your medical records, and act as your durable power of attorney for finances;"

It's like, yes! We have got to do all the things, prepare for all the stuffs, be ready to feel all the feels – and if we're smart, we'll start doing it now! We cannot go blindly into our last inning thinking it will all "just work out," which is precisely how my father pursued his journey. And though his Golden Years did "just work out" better than most, it was a risky course. He just got lucky. People have been shouting this from the hilltops for a long time, yet so few of us decide to listen. I will go

on a heretical limb and express that Moses' bestselling Ten Command-
ments are among the first and most fundamental compilations of good
grand planning. Let me list (and add current context to) a few, and you
let that simmer a minute:

- "Thou shalt not take the name of the Lord thy God in vain."
  Minimizing yourself and your stuff reduces your family's opportunity for cussing and taking the Lord's name in vain out of
  frustration, anger, and desperation.

- "Remember the sabbath day, to keep it holy." Establishing and
  staying connected to a community, like the church home that
  you haven't been to in years, is healthy and an important place
  to find good support as you age.

- "Honor thy father and thy mother." Trust and good communication are the foundation of a strong family.

- "Thou shalt not kill." Relinquish the keys before you do —
  actually — kill someone.

It's a stretch. But there's a connection! From a spiritual perspective,
both a grand plan and most religious tenets – including the Ten Com-
mandments – advocate a lessening of self and flexing empathy, compassion, and a "doing unto others" mentality. This is a critical piece of
the puzzle.

Of course, preparing for our senior years is not a faith-based concern;
however, religious texts offer some wisdom and best practices. Like this
scripture regarding the stupidity of hoarding stuff and storage and all
the things we value: "Don't store up for yourselves treasures on earth,
where moth and rust destroy and where thieves break in and steal. But
store up for yourselves treasures in heaven, where neither moth nor
rust destroys and where thieves don't break in and steal. For where
your treasure is, there your heart will be also." Matthew 6:19-2.

Buddhists practice Maranasati, the mindfulness of death and death
awareness. By getting comfortable with images of corpses and imagery
of death and decay in contemplating the nine stages of a decaying

corpse, Buddhists understand the fullness and natural process of aging and dying. As a result, they are not afraid of either outcome and instead see age as an imminent, "non-improvable" human condition – they are comfortable with and accepting of death. Imagine if every aging person had this perspective! I think we'd be much less stressed about dying if we were better on board with the concept of our mortality. Plastic surgeons would be a thing of the past like any industry selling older adults "youthful" appearances, products, and styles. We wouldn't take life so seriously if we could never forget dying is imminent.

Most religious teachings – including Judaism, Hinduism, Islam, and Christianity – are big proponents of looking after, respecting, and taking responsibility for elderly family members, including multigenerational housing arrangements. This thinking is also a significant consideration in grand planning, which encourages communication and trust with family members and open conversation about housing needs, abilities, and expectations. Another big theme in most world religions is respecting seniors for their wisdom, experience, and mastery and encouraging elders to become teachers and examples for the younger generation. Both practices are essential to mitigating geri-drama during our older years, yet they are often dismissed today.

Author Michael Hebb discusses the need for conversation, clarity of outcomes, and planning in his book *Let's Talk About Death Over Dinner*, which is also required reading for this grand planning challenge.

"If doctors and nurses had clear direction from each of us – advance-care directives, clear power of attorney, healthcare proxy – and if our families knew our wishes for the type of care we want at our life's end if they knew what we want to happen to our body and how we want to be celebrated, the emotional and financial burden would significantly reduce."

I agree, and so do most thoughtful, planful people – especially the ones who have gone through end-of-life geri-fiascos and come out the other side determined to stir change for themselves and their loved ones.

One of the biggest hurdles to it all is the intersection between physical well-being and happiness, and the be-all-end-all expert in this is Dr. Atul Gawande, author of *Being Mortal*. And again, the delta in this equation is whether or not folks are having honest conversations – or healthy real talk – about it.

"We think our job is to ensure health and survival. But really, it is larger than that. It is to enable well-being. Well-being is about the reasons one wishes to be alive. Those reasons matter not just at the end of life, or when debility comes, but all along the way," Gawande says in his bestselling book. "Whenever serious sickness or injury strikes and your body or mind breaks down, the vital questions are the same: What is your understanding of the situation and its potential outcomes? What are your fears, and what are your hopes? What trade-offs are you willing to make and not willing to make? And what is the course of action that best serves this understanding?"

The course of action is making a Grand Plan – whatever that looks like to you and the people supporting you on that walk during your final inning. So, let's get back to those steps now.

Part II: Soft Steps — the "Shoulds"

STEP 10: EMBRACE YOUR AGE, APPEARANCE AND ROLE.

THE PROBLEM, IN REAL **talk:**

Many seniors flat-out refuse to accept their age, stage, and natural physical state as they age. This leads to an unhealthy obsession with appearance and a reluctance to engage in some of the more expected senior roles, such as grandparenting, shepherding, counseling, and unconditional loving. This denial results in unnecessary beauty maintenance costs (read expensive plastic surgery, injections, regimens, and apparel), unaligned perceptions of self-worth, and a breakdown in family relationships because everyone's expectations are out of whack.

If you've ever said, "I'm not old," or "I don't want to live there, with all those OLD people," or "I don't like being around icky old people" (as if you, yourself, are not close in age by any measure), you are making the divide between yourself and reality unreasonably broad. This mindset is exclusionary. It is divisive. This is narcissism talking, and it's not a good look.

In the book *Two Old Broads: Stuff You Need to Know That You Didn't Know You Needed to Know,* authors M.E. Hecht and Whoopi Goldberg call growing old growing UP. That's a great concept. Instead of I'm not old, try "I'm growing up."

The biggest problem, however, is how these contradictions create a barrier to critical grand planning. You need to look at yourself honestly and acknowledge you are getting older and approaching the last inning of your life game to ensure you are adequately prepared for all the curve balls coming your way. You will strike out. You will lose.

"Becoming elderly often takes us by surprise," said Linda K Stroh, Ph .D., and Karen K. Brees, Ph.D., in their book *Getting Real About Getting Older.* "Unlike other stages of life, we have done little to prepare for this one. It's clear with other stages of life that we literally take on a new identity – of spouse or partner, parent, new brand manager, shift supervisor, doctor, lawyer, factory worker. Most of us, however, are not aware that we have a new identity or need to create one as we become older."

The solution IMHO:

This is another easy answer that only requires a little action. In fact, the answer should be liberating – a relief, hopefully! To be more accepting of your age, stage, and physical state, you have to nod your head in agreement, love yourself and who you've become, let go of silly expectations, and go with the flow. We can all do that, right?

Regarding your appearance, do NOT be a victim of some unrealistic version of beauty today's culture puts on you and the rest of us. Plumper lips, spackled crow's feet, tightened turkey necks, and expensive Barbie-toned hairdos do not make you a more attractive person. Beauty comes from inner confidence, free and accessible to all of us. Invest a little time and practice in flexing that muscle – the one that sharpens personal satisfaction with yourself as you are in this moment.

My Dad's mom, Clinton Wright Walker Person, went by the name Grandmother, and she had such muscle tone. She was one bad betch, one I hope to be like as I dance toward my golden years. Why? Well, for one, she looked like a grandmother. She wore cardigan sweaters with balls of tissue paper in her sleeves and cooked goulash when she came to visit. She got a permanent every so often, and her only beauty product was a thick (THICK) slathering of Ponds night cream. Grandmother smelled richly of talcum powder. She was beautiful and approachable in every way to me, and that's the kind of Me-maw I plan to be one day.

Also, she never demanded an audience; she was OK to be quiet and intentional and present, which manifested as pure, unconditional love for us envelope-pushing grandkids. These qualities, too, are on my list. She was quick to pray for you — and write letters. This wasn't very pleasant sometimes, but I miss these things now. Plus, she kept her life simple and non-glam and small town. Totally hip, I think.

The biggest kicker was Grandmother's go-with-the-flowness. When the time was right, she moved from her "big house" to a small two-bed-room condo in Goliad, Texas. When the time was even better, she happily packed up a few things and moved to an elder care community in San Antonio without fanfare or disagreement. And it was a gift having her so close; I remember it well. It's *bougie bad and thick to be Grand-motherly, I think! Grandmothercore is a lovely aesthetic.*

That's not to say you can't or shouldn't enjoy looking nice or wearing clothing that flatters. For some people, and I speak for myself here, clothing and style is a hobby that checks major boxes in the creativity department. Keep doing that if it makes you happy; just don't get obsessed over it, or base an image or role on that material vision. Love yourself in its natural state first and foremost.

Let's talk about accepting your age. I don't mean to say you should look at yourself in the mirror and scream, "I'm so old, I'm freaking 75 years old! Woe is me!" then go about your day expecting to act in a way that is doddering or old-fashioned or some frail, concocted version of what society thinks a 75-year-old should look and feel like. No, that's dumb. That belief is totally unhealthy and super unrealistic. When we talk about age acceptance, it's more about acknowledging where you are in life and less about how you look or feel. When you look in that mirror, try smiling at yourself, nodding at your image, and saying, "This is 75 – I'm effing proud of myself and where I am in life at this moment." You are still going with the flow and showing love to yourself, but you are also acknowledging where you are on your sunset stroll. Acknowledging is important. Acknowledging leaves the door open to grand planning.

So, you've accepted your appearance and age; now pat yourself on the back and make sure the old shoe that's been lugging you around all these years knows you see all that hard work it's been putting in on your behalf. Your physical abilities are what they are, and you've done well. Keep taking care of your body and exercising it to a comfortable capacity. Feed it healthy food and treat it with respect. But stop putting unrealistic expectations on your aging body. The things you could do when you were in your 20s are activities you can handle with a different ease today. Believe that, and you're sure to bust a hip or need one of those "I've fallen, and I can't get up" devices around your neck. Be easy on the old girl (or boy[LP2])! Love her for all she's provided you!

In addition to creating a more conducive environment for grand planning, acknowledging all these realities also helps shape your elder roles. By that, I mean the more venerable life positions like being a grandparent, a family matriarch, or a teacher. When you cannot be realistic about your elderly status, you will miss out on these important responsibilities. If you say BS like "I'm not old" and are so tightened up by plastic surgery that you cannot smile properly, you won't find the joy in being a grandparent or a patriarch because, by their very wording, grandparent and patriarch indicate you are getting older...and you are NOT old, remember? Sigh.

Grandparenting and sharing life experiences and lessons with those younger than you can be rewarding activities. You can pass down all the incredible knowledge and ah-ha moments you've experienced with people who can benefit from your unique strengths. When you can engage in it and put your heart into it—without fear of being considered OLD – you will benefit from stronger connections with your family, a bigger capacity to love, the satisfaction of "passing on" your carefully curated strengths to future generations and, most importantly, from the returned support of family and friends when you need extra support on your senior stroll. As rewarding as embracing these elder roles can be, it also is a smart and strategic move: the family and friends with whom you are now well connected are much more likely to support you in the execution of your life's Grand Plan. You need these folks as much as they need and want you – acknowledge that and win!

There are so many strengths we can embrace as elder adults that can redefine our sunset stroll as a beautiful, empowering phase of life that offers unique opportunities for growth and fulfillment. We can celebrate:

- Wisdom and experience

- Inner peace and acceptance

- More time for reflection on our journey

- Gratitude for life!

- New opportunities that may be just around the corner

- Stronger relationships with family and friends who are at different stages of life

- Self-reinvention

- The joy of building a legacy and watching it unfold

Embracing old age is not about denying the challenges that come with it but instead accepting and celebrating the unique gifts it brings.

Helpful resources:

The Swedish Art of Aging Exuberantly: Life Wisdom from Someone Who Will (Probably) Die Before You by Margareta Magnusson

From Strength to Strength: Finding Success, Happiness and Deep Purpose in the Second Half of Life by Arthur C. Brooks

Two Old Broads: Stuff You Need to Know That You Didn't Know You Needed to Know by M.E. Hecht and Whoopi Goldberg

The Mindful Grandparent by Marilyn McEntyre and Shirley Showalter

Nanaville: Adventures in Grandparenting by Anna Quindlen

Grand: A Grandparent's Wisdom for a Happy Life by Charles Johnson

Finding Meaning in the Second Half of Life: How to Finally, Really Grow Up by James Hollis

Getting Real About Getting Older by Linda K Stroh PhD and Karen K. Brees PhD

Honest Aging: An Insider's Guide to the Second Half of Life by Rosanne M. Leipzig MD PhD

STEP 11: FOCUS ON YOUR MIND, BODY AND SOUL.

THE PROBLEM, IN REAL **talk:**

Taking care of ourselves — mind, body, and soul — is the trifecta core of a geri-life and something we should pay special attention to as we set out on the sunset stroll. Yet, few of us are. A 2023 study from the Public Religion Research Institute (PRRI) showed just 16 percent of Americans surveyed said religion is the most essential thing in their lives, down from 20 percent a decade ago. A 2022 study from the National Center for Health Statistics indicated that only 10.3 percent of women and 15.3 percent of men over 65 met the 2018 Physical Activity Guidelines for Americans for aerobic and muscle-strengthening activities. And according to the National Council on Aging, between 25-30 percent of older adults in the U.S. — that's roughly 20 million people, folks! — have reported mental health disorders since April 2020. The most frightening statistic is from the U.S. Substance Abuse and Mental Health Services Administration and the National Academy of Medicine, which found less than 50 percent of older adults with mental or substance user disorders receive treatment.

In short, we are not caring for ourselves or seeking help for our minds, bodies, and souls as we should be.

That means we are losing ground on opportunities to feel and function better, think and respond to life more sanely, and thrive in environments with built-in resources for support, community, and transcendental experiences as we age.

The solution IMHO:

This topic can be deep and complicated. Let's keep things simple and easy to digest and not get too science-y on this topic. Most of the answers here are pretty duh, with a little practical application going a long way.

Let's start with the body party of the mind-body-soul equation. To pursue a healthy body, we need only consider ways to take care of the old station wagon that's been getting us around all these years. Our physical vessels run better when used, have good gas in the tank, and receive periodic maintenance. So, we should exercise daily, eat well instead of polluting ourselves with toxic substances, and manage our health via doctors' appointments, treatments, and medication. That's it on the body front.

If we do just a little of that, the results will significantly impact our existence. A recent National Center for Health Statistics study found that "regular physical activity can improve overall health and prevent negative health outcomes in people of all ages (1). Increasing the proportion of adults meeting the 2018 Physical Activity Guidelines for Americans for aerobic and muscle-strengthening activities is a Healthy People 2030 Leading Health Indicator (2), highlighting its priority for well-being. Research shows that health benefits occur with at least 150 minutes a week of moderate-intensity aerobic activity and that both aerobic and muscle-strengthening activities are beneficial."

According to the Centers for Disease Control and Prevention, "all older adults – both men and women – can benefit from regular moderate physical activities...even for people with medical conditions such as arthritis, heart disease, obesity, and high blood pressure."

According to the National Council on Aging, other key benefits of exercise include:

- The prevention of bone loss.

- The relief of osteoarthritis pain.

- The prevention of chronic disease.

- A boost in immunity.

- Mood improvement.

The NCOA suggests older adults "incorporate a blend of aerobic exercise, strength/resistance training, and stretching/flexibility exercises." That is a LOT of benefits for a small investment of time and energy.

Good nutrition and medical upkeep are also simple math. As for what you put in your body, try to eat a variety of fresh, clean, unprocessed foods as much as possible and consume the bad stuff in moderation. Drink a lot of water. And don't overdo it on the alcohol and such. Get plenty of rest. ("Get at least eight hours of beauty sleep, nine if you're ugly," according to Betty White, lol.) Take the vitamins and medications your doctor tells you to take and get an annual exam on the books every year.

Wise food choices and ongoing medical care have big physical payoffs. An Abbott nutrition care program study of 600 malnourished or at-risk adults who followed a personalized nutrition program resulted in an 84 percent increase in participants' psychological well-being, a 76 percent increase in quality of life, a 75 percent increase in cognition, and a 48 percent increase in physical functionality. The National Institute on Aging quoted a 2021 study that showed "regular check-ups help doctors catch chronic diseases early and can help patients reduce risk factors for disease, such as high blood pressure and cholesterol levels. People who went to the doctor regularly reported improved quality of life and wellness.

Like Richard Simmons says: "Work hard and take care of yourself, and you'll be just fine." Easy peasy. Box checked.

Now, let's move to the spirituality and religion leg of the geri-health stool. I think this one is fascinating – and practical. And more competent people have many encouraging things to say about honing your faith practices and community.

A Merck study by Daniel B. Kaplan Ph.D. called "Religion and Spirituality in Older People" determined that "People who are religious tend to have better physical and mental health than nonreligious people" and said religion seems to have many benefits on mental health, physical and social functioning, and caregiving. Another study from the National Institutes of Health sampled 3,968 community-dwelling adults aged 64-101 in the Piedmont area of North Carolina. It concluded that "older adults, particularly women, who attended religious services at least once a week appear to have a survival advantage over those attending services less frequently."

Dr. Samuel White III, author of *Aging Gracefully: Spiritual Care for Aging Adults,* calls a spiritual perspective on aging good for personal transformation and something akin to "medicine for longevity and health."

"Research shows that people with an active involvement in church or spiritual community live on average seven years longer than those who do not," White said. Seven years! Wow!

Why is that, you wonder? My limited knowledge reveals a multilayered answer, but it generally inspires healthy thought and a supportive community. Churches, synagogues, mosques, yoga dens, meditation groups, and other places of worship consistently gather people of all ages – at least once a week, if not more. That's a familiar group of humans who look out for each other, notice inconsistencies, and seek ways to help each other.

Again, I point to my sweet neighborhood friend Suzanne on this. She and her husband have made a tremendous investment in community and outreach at church. So much so that when they were down with temporary disabilities, their church and neighborhood friends surrounded them with the support they needed to make it over the hump.

In *Getting Real About Getting Older* by Linda K. Stroh, Ph.D., and Karen K. Brees, Ph.D., the authors talk about the social importance of religious organizations.

"They provide emotional support, care for physical needs, and provide opportunities for socializing and volunteering. These functions become increasingly important as we grow older and find our youthful independence and good health eroding," Brees and Stroh wrote in their essential manual. "It's inevitable, then, that at some point we will need to rely more and more on others, and often our religious choices fill that need, putting us in close contact with like-minded people who are oriented toward helping others within their community. It's true that there's safety in numbers."

Lastly, on the faith and spirituality front, let me quickly plug in the helpful "others-focused-ness" these communities provide geri-humans.

"When you spend serious time and effort focused on transcendental things, it puts your little world into proper context and takes the focus off yourself. Most of our days, I am thinking me, me, me. It's like watching the same dreary television show, over and over, all day long. It's so boring," wrote author Arthur C. Brooks, in his New York Times bestseller *From Strength to Strength: Finding Success, Happiness and Deep Purpose in the Second Half of Life*. "Faith forces me into the cosmos to consider the source of truth, the origin of life, and the good of others. This focus brings refreshment and relief."

Regarding the final part of the mind-body-health geri-trifecta, the mind – or, in more applicable terms, our mental health- is the hardest. It's the hardest because there's no hard and fast answer for strengthening this muscle. There isn't an easy practice like "shop on the perimeter of the grocery store" or "eat an apple a day to keep the doctor away." The mind is a complex bundle of neurons fueled by mystery and question marks. I'm not sure we know exactly how it works.

We know it's wise to keep it running by challenging it with problems, information, games, learning, and experiences. Part of the prescription for a healthy mind is to read more – to solve more crossword puzzles, jumbles, and equations. The other bit is to be honest about your cognition and brain function and to be open to the observations of those close to you. Many mind thieves like dementia and Alzheimer's can be mitigated by listening to our loved ones and seeking help initially. Mental health resources are available for many challenges if we pursue them.

Effective mind, body, and soul care requires flexing the mind, exercising social engagement, meditating and being mindful, learning for life, exercising your body, maintaining a healthy and balanced diet, resting and sleeping according to your body's needs, exploring and strengthening your spiritual practices, volunteering, embracing creativity, and maintaining positive relationships that lift your spirits and bring joy to your life.

When considering your Grand Plan for geri-success, put your mind, body, and soul into it and solicit honest feedback from the people you love.

Helpful resources

The Gift of Years Joan Chittister

Aging Gracefully: Spiritual Care for Aging Adults by Dr. Samuel White III

Getting Real About Getting Older Linda K. Stroh PhD and Karen K. Brees PhD

From Strength to Strength: Finding Success, Happiness and Deep Purpose in the Second Half of Life by Arthur C. Brooks

Step 12: Communicate with your people, early and honestly and often.

THE PROBLEM, IN REAL **talk:**

If I could relay the single biggest WTAF? complaint from Gen-X care-givers and geri-drama-experienced adults, it would be the reluctance of loved ones to communicate openly and honestly about topics of grand planning. I'm talking about the dreaded "I-Don't-Wanna-Talk-About-Its." Worse, it's known as "The Nunyas," as in, it's none of your business. This black hole of communication causes big trouble in families and care management situations. At best, it elicits major eye-rolls at the family dinner table and sidebar text conversations you're not included in that begin with "seriously?!" At worst, it crushes dreams and reframes our visions of the future. When expectations are not in alignment or elder adults plan in a void, the people we love get hurt.

I don't know why this non-communication occurs regularly during human experience. Generally, we are a pretty prepared people. As soon as we think about getting pregnant, we buy books on what to expect when we're expecting. When babies come, parents study articles and guides on how to raise them and what resources are necessary to sustain them. Later, we might involve therapists, counselors, and caregivers to manage a plan for our children's best outcomes. We talk to our spouses, family, and friends about how to save money for their futures – how we will pay for their education, life experiences, health care, insurance, and change-making expenses like bikes, cars, and travel. We save money to pay for their weddings and steer them toward making wise choices in their schooling, careers, and life by engaging in healthy banter about it all. Later, when these children become adults and begin their own lives, they start the same conversations with their people about best practices for #winning at Adulting 401 and beyond.

Then, there's this weird void. As we become older adults, the conversation about life comes to a strange, screeching halt. Gone are the shelves full of self-help books, the healthy dinner table discussions about the next steps, and the peer knowledge about professional resources, tools, and providers. It's like everyone shuts up about it all. And I'm here to tell you, this is a terrible, no good, very bad thing.

Here are a few examples of what often happens next:

- Since you didn't save much for retirement and long-term care during the pre-geri-years, you decided (but never told anyone) you'd move in with one of your adult children when the going got tough. When it did, your adult kids were totally unprepared for the expense, time commitment, and physical assistance needs of this unplanned living arrangement. Consequently, they became resentful because they now had to spend their paychecks, savings, and retirement kitty on YOU and your bad planning.

- After watching a friend die on a ventilator, you decided you'd never want to be on some machine during your darkest hour. That will NEVER be me, you tell yourself – and only yourself. But later, when you have an accident and get hooked up to one of those damn devices you'd hoped to avoid, there you languish – for a long, long time – because you never told anyone this life support machine business wasn't going to be part of your plan, and your kids think you deserve a better chance (thoughts and prayers!) at regaining consciousness. Sadly, that never happens, but thank God you're alive on that machine.

- You don't give a flip about having a funeral and hope your kids don't make a big to-do about it all when you're gone. Having been to so many overblown adios moments during your lifetime, you have visions of a simple cremation with no function or fanfare attached because that's how you roll. But you forget to tell your people these essential facts, and when you finally pass, the worst thing ever happens. Though you'll never know it, your kids do dumb sh** like buy the white laminated casket and invite all the people you DGAS about anymore to regale the legacy you always wished would remain private, perfectly on the down low, and cheap as hell.

In my experience, the consequences of non-talk could have been much worse, and I am grateful they weren't. My father, an attorney by trade, was well prepared with his legal documents – the durable power of attorney papers, medical directives, estate planning directions, and health care surrogacy – before he ended up unexpectedly in the hospital with double pneumonia in 2021. We were all squared away there, and that was a tremendous relief. Over the years, he also talked to us loosely about how he wanted things to go down should a medical emergency come his way, so we felt good knowing his "wishes" on a few critical decisions. But we were completely unprepared for all the gray areas when discussing whether to remove someone from life support. In most cases, doctors won't tell you there's a 100 percent chance someone will die – there's conjecture, chance, and possibility with every medical decision. A more dedicated and detailed conversation with my Dad ahead of time would have helped remove the grey from these equations.

My father was also highly reluctant to discuss financial matters of any kind. For decades, my brother and I had little insight into whether he had adequately prepared for the expenses and unknowns of his senior experience. When we asked him, direct questions were always met with a pat "it's all going to work out" or "I'm just fine" answers. This closed conversation caused me great anxiety and led my husband and I to make ghosty financial plans based on whether we might support Dad in his later years. It was hugely disconcerting. And at the end of the day, it was all unnecessary angst because he was "just fine" after all. But a little open dialogue would have gone a long way.

I imagine the big problem is that we are reluctant to talk about our mortality. Death and dying are scary. It's not something people generally talk about at cocktail parties because it makes people feel uncomfortable. But it's one of the most essential, life-giving things we can do for ourselves, our friends, and our family. It's one of the most fundamental parts of a workable grand plan.

The solution IMHO:

There's only one way to solve this problem: to START TALKING ABOUT OUR MORTALITY – and all fears, concerns, plans, and dreams associated – with more people in our orbit who aren't named us.

Be an open book. Overshare. Be the devil in the details. Talk until you see ears bleeding.

My most urgent suggestion is that no topic is off-limits and that all conversations happen openly, honestly, and regularly. Adult children should be privy to their parents' financial records at an early age. No financial matters should be a surprise or be revealed during a gaspy last-will-and-testament-reading as they do in the movies. This should be straight up, easily accessible, nuts and bolts intel. Medical prefer-ences should be discussed frequently, especially as they evolve over time. Your people should know your business – what doctors you see, where you stash your medical, legal, and financial records, who your accountant is, where your investments are, and who services your home, car, and businesses. Show them your provider lists. Share your passwords. Talk about it – all.

Recently, I read Michael Hebb's bestselling book *Let's Talk About Death (Over Dinner)*. I encourage anyone and everyone to read this book, as it puts this whole conversation thing in perspective.

"We're a little messed up about death, to put it bluntly," Hebb says in his book's first few pages. "On the one hand, it's all around us. We flock to dark cable dramas and slow down our cars out of morbid fascination with traffic accidents. But to talk about it with one another? Honestly and openly? Forget it. When we live within this contradiction, we lose the chance for connection, communication, healing, and the richness and value that can come from facing our mortality head-on."

Hebb prescribes dinner events with family and friends during which guests honestly explore questions about death. Each chapter is a prompt and includes his experiences with people answering them. His questions include: If you had only thirty days left to live, how would you spend them? Your last day? Your last hour? How do you talk to kids about death? Do you believe in an afterlife? What would you want people to say about you at your funeral? So many more get my brain working; you must borrow or purchase this book and see how it inspires you and the conversations you're willing to have with your family and friends.

Hebb and many other brave writers who share their experiences with death and post-death are spot on in their intentions: talking about it is healing work. Other great books that push this agenda include Katy Butler's *The Art of Dying Well: A Practical Guide to a Good End of Life* and *Knocking on Heaven's Door*, and Margareta Magnusson's *The Swedish Art of Aging Exuberantly* and *The Swedish Art of Death Cleaning*. These are all excellent, perspective-filling reads.

Another helpful resource is Five Wishes, an extremely helpful booklet that helps adults lay out their wants and needs as death approaches. According to the Five Wishes website fivewishes.org, Five Wishes was developed as "the first advance care plan to address personal, emotional, and spiritual wishes in addition to medical treatment. It's called 'the living will with heart and soul' because we've based our document on what is most important – being able to define a roadmap for how you want to be cared for." The booklet was made with consultation from the American Bar Association and end-of-life experts and with the support of the Robert Wood Johnson Foundation. "It is a comprehensive, person-centered advance care planning program that offers a proven, easy-to-use approach to having effective and compassionate conversations." The Five Wishes booklet is available at a low cost online for individuals and groups at agingwithdignity.org or fivewishes.org. Good conversations are behind this process in a big way.

In the manual *How to Care for Aging Parents,* author Virginia Morris describes the conversation piece of the care puzzle as "critical." She says there is always time to talk to parents and siblings about the future.

"Don't put this off. Talk with your parents and, depending on the situation, hold a family meeting to discuss your parents' current care and future needs," Morris said. "Assign jobs, sort out finances, and plan for what care he will need as he grows more frail. For your parent, planning ensures that he has a say in his future, it affords him more choices, and it gives him time to prepare for change...Do it now because it is much, *much* easier to have these discussions when there is no dire problem at hand when you are talking about some distant possibility when it's a matter of "What if..."...Talk now; you'll be glad you did."

She said the subjects of money and death make people uncomfortable, but it's essential to have them.

"Keep in mind that talking about the worst-case scenarios won't make them come true, and refusing to talk about them won't make them go away," Morris said in her book. "Ignoring the inevitable will only leave you unprepared for a crisis that will almost surely one day come."

Our mortality and that of our loved ones should not shock us. We should expect it, plan for it, and celebrate it — and most of all, we should begin honest conversations about it.

Helpful resources

How to Care for Aging Parents by Virginia Morris

The Art of Dying Well: A Practical Guide to a Good End of Life, by Katy Butler

Five Wishes by Aging with Dignity

Step 13: Trust the people who love you.

THE PROBLEM, IN REAL **talk:**

Whether it's due to fear or panic or legitimate concern, elderly adults often think they can't trust – or know better than – the people who are on their care front lines. Those special somebodies may be adult children, grandchildren, close longtime friends, neighbors, or professionals. But whoever they are, their advice or direction is totes sus, as in suspicious. They are not to be trusted. They come bearing fake news. This lack of trust is a mistake and makes sticky situations even stickier.

The solution IMHO:

Spoiler alert: the top two most important steps of a perfect Grand Plan are communication, which we've discussed, and trust. Trust may be the biggest.

With honest conversations about future caregiving, expectations, and everyone's hopes for senior living, people are less likely to feel side-swiped or unprepared. Conversations should begin in midlife, when it's hardly a tomorrow or right now thing — and continue in everyday chatter moving forward. There's some work involved in the conversation.

Trust, however, is the easy, no-thinking part. You raised or surrounded yourself with a few good, loving people during your life who want only the best for you. So, when that grown-up twirp you adore makes a suggestion about your planning or caregiving or physical and emotional needs, trust that kid. Trust the opinion of that best friend who may see something you don't want to acknowledge. Communication and trust are the keys we set down in the house somewhere and can't for the life of us find.

If my kids can dig around through rock-hard dirt clods in the sweltering Arkansas summer heat to find that Crater of Diamonds mother lode (a regular occurrence in their childhood), I can undoubtedly dig down into the core of my pride and aging obstinance and flimsy ego and do what my people tell me is best for me, my circumstances, or my family. I love and trust these kiddos deeply. I refuse to let age skew that relationship.

I look forward to them telling me what makes sense. That sounds like such relief; I am totally down with it all. Down through the dirt clods to what sounds like a real treasure of a Grand Plan.

Helpful Resources:

Boundaries: When to Say Yes, How to Say No to Take Control of Your Life, by Dr. Henry Cloud and Dr. John Townsend.

Eldercare mediation and counseling services

AARP Caregiving Resource Center

National Center on Elder Abuse (NCEA)

The 5 Love Languages: The Secret to Love That Lasts, by Gary Chapman.

Local senior support groups and community centers

STEP 14: ESTABLISH, BUILD AND STAY CONNECTED TO A RELIABLE, LOVING, ACCESSIBLE COMMUNITY — PICK "YOUR PERSON OR PEOPLE."

THE PROBLEM, IN REAL **talk:**

Loneliness and isolation can be debilitating during the sunset stroll. Without a close community that provides connection, engagement, and support, even self-sufficient seniors can find themselves in a real jam. In the United States, this condition is near epidemic. According to a 2020 Pew Research study, 27 percent of adults ages 60 and older live alone, compared with 16 percent of adults in the 130 countries and territories studied. That's a lot of being alone! As humans, we weren't meant to live like that — we need our people! Senior needs can go unaddressed without community, leaving super unhealthy, crisis-building scenarios to fester. This is a significant problem.

Speaking of our people, we aren't adopting them and senior planning with them how we should as we age. There is a dearth of conversation around imagining who "that person" or "those people" will be should we become infirm or lose our ability to manage ourselves. And in so many cases, that choice is made during a crisis or in now-mode, which is never the right way to approach our Golden Year glory. We need a person or people we trust to step in lovingly during our pothole moments and help us make the best decisions for us. When there's no person, our future – finances, health care, everything – is jeopardized and left to chance.

The solution IMHO:

One-day-geri-friends, take note. The best solution to this problem is just like the other 20, which is to be aware of it and talk to your people about it – openly and often.

Let's start with the community part of this equation. This issue can often be resolved organically. You may have always enjoyed the community at church or a restaurant you frequent – maybe you find it at the grocery store or on morning walks in your neighborhood. Perhaps your community includes the playgroup mom friends you made long ago who still live around the corner. Maybe it's your family – your adult kids or nieces and nephews who now live and work in a neighborhood nearby. We're not talking about reinventing the wheel here. Your community likely exists today in a very healthy condition. The challenge in that case is to maintain or re-establish it. Go back to church if you haven't been in a while. Make sure there's peace and a healthy relationship with your family and friends – the ones who will rescue you from geri-disaster.

If life has changed and you're no longer connected to the groups, venues, and activities providing you with connection points and engagement, a much different task is ahead. In this case, you need to go out and build a new community – it is imperative to make this effort, so you should start it now. That may mean developing an old hobby or joining a new worship community. Or maybe you get involved in a cause issue or activity that brings people from your neighborhood together. And if you don't have family or good friends nearby, or you don't know them well or feel very connected to them, start building those relationships. Start making plans with that niece who lives across town – invite her over for supper and make yourself a resource. Initiate a daily walk, coffee gathering, or book club with someone who moved across the street. Put yourself out there, friend! Put heart and soul into your people currency – new or renewed!

These connections are meaningful because one day, you will depend on them. Plus, it's good for your health! A September 2019 article in the online blog Healthline shared research from the National Institute on Aging, which showed community – being social, more specifically – has many mental and physical health benefits, including reduction of dementia development, high blood pressure, heart disease, obesity, depression, cognitive decline, Alzheimer's disease, and more. A statistic from the same study in the Healthline article indicated that 60-year-olds who visited with friends daily were 12 percent less likely to develop dementia than those who only saw one or two friends every few months.

Again, my friend, Suzanne, is a great example of working this resource. She and her husband moved to our neighborhood a decade or more ago and immediately made themselves the center of our community. They hosted neighborhood potluck suppers, staged fundraisers for organizations dear to people nearby, gathered folks for Bible studies and community events, and dug deep into building relationships at their church. These folks even went so far as to "adopt" parentless parents and "stray" children as their own, providing temporary housing, hospitality, and unconditional love.

When Suzanne had knee replacement surgery and Joe was admitted to the hospital unexpectedly – and when their life was paralyzed for a spell – you can imagine what that community did in return. People around the neighborhood stepped in with meal deliveries and offered to drive. Suzanne said one neighbor just decided she would come to the house every day to just be – just in case. That's the payoff of community and why it's so important to build it.

Let's talk quickly about picking "a person." While collecting community is critical to our senior health and well-being, designating at least one person to look after your best interests in an official capacity is critical. By "picking a person," I mean thinking about someone or a few people in your life who you can count on and, at some point, SIGN on as your legal advocate – your Dual Power of Attorney, your Medical Power of Attorney, your healthcare proxy, the executor of your estate, your fiduciary, your trusted advisor. It would be best if you had someone who can officially step in and care for you when your cookies crumble (which they will, and always when you least expect it.) And once you pick that person or people, select a backup or two – just in case.

Once again, the process of people-picking begins with conversation that happens openly and often. And it starts with an ask. Whether it's one or all of your children, a special nephew, or a close younger friend you trust, your person is first owed the courtesy of conference – and at the very least, messaging that they have been chosen as your "person."

The older couple for whom I helped arrange care and management forgot to tell me I was their person, whoops! They did not have children or family on their scene but knew my father and me back in my childhood – we're talking nearly 40 years ago. At some point, they did the brilliant thing of setting up their legal documents and picking their people – my Dad and me (though we were not part of their inner circle) – but neglected to inform us of our roles. When the housekeeper on their scene started calling me with strange reports of deplorable circumstances, I had my shoulders by my ears with my hands in the air like, "What do you want me to do about that?" until a call from their lawyer revealed my long-hidden part in their gordian-knot puzzle. Of course, that was all the least of my worries moving forward, but it sure would have been nice – to know.

I digress with boring pity-party sentiments, but this kind of non-communication baloney happens ALL THE TIME to people I've spoken to during the past year. It's such a simple act, yet it is so hard for folks for some reason! With just a little conversation and awareness, geri-drama almost always becomes a non-issue.

During conversations with your person, it's good to be open and honest about the expectations in this relationship. For instance, if you are determined to never, ever be subjected to a ventilator or chest-crushing revival compression, then say so – over and over again, so there is no doubt in your person's mind what they should do in that case. Your person also should feel free to share their limits. For example, they might say, "Look, I'm not going to put up with any BS if you have dementia or aren't acting reasonably or refusing to do the right thing; I'm going to help you do the right thing no matter what – just so you know." That kind of frank talk will be helpful when you ARE acting out, fighting the system, or being a stone in the stream. I promise your person will feel better about pushing you toward safe, sane, practical behavior. Please ensure the person you trust and have chosen feels confident they are well equipped to manage your life in a way that feels right for both of you.

Creating and sustaining your community is life-giving! It brings us social connection, emotional support, physical health, mental stimulation, and opportunities for continued learning and personal growth. When we're in a good community, we are safer and more secure, have a sense of purpose, and have access to resources we wouldn't have if we were stuck at home – alone and angry and unfulfilled.

The connections we form within the communities we build for ourselves create a sense of belonging, camaraderie, and a high quality of life. Get yourself some and live better!

Helpful resources

Honest Aging: An Insider's Guide to the Second Half of Life by Rosanne M. Leipzig MD PhD

Getting Real About Getting Older by Linda K Stroh PhD and Karen K. Brees PhD

The Gift of Years by Joan Chittister

STEP 15: BE RELEVANT AND KEEP UP WITH KEY TECHNOLOGY.

THE PROBLEM, IN REAL **talk:**

I can be short and sweet on this one. If you're not keeping up with technology, you are missing out on some very big, meaningful moments, including opportunities to make your life easier, healthier, and safer; information that will bolster and better connect you to family and friends; and occasions to learn, challenge your mental acuity and be entertained.

The solution IMHO:

The most straightforward answer here is to stay fluent in technologies that people in your sphere actively use or promote. That doesn't mean going out and downloading every social media app or streaming channel; it doesn't mean wasting money on new gadgets. It simply means keeping up with communication, social, and management technology most average people use.

Here's a what NOT to do example. A friend's mother has always struggled in this area and fought valiantly to avoid practical use of literally EVERYTHING that makes life easier today: the computer, email, internet cellular phone, movie and book downloads, smart television, cable, social media, and the microwave, even.

Oh, she also gave a Heisman to hearing aids because...what? Who needs those anyway? Too complicated. You can imagine what kind of nonsense has ensued over the years trying to stay in touch at a bare minimum. When she doesn't pick up (i.e., hear) the landline squawking, my friend has to get in his car and drive over to ensure she's OK. It's what headaches are made of!

This technology ignorance affected others big time: No Wi-Fi means no ability to install communication or security technology or "I've fallen and I can't get up" assistance; no social media indicates she's not keeping up with family events on the line; no internet means no good television or movies to watch during her long, lonely days and no Ancestry.com to get obsessed over; and no smartphone means no picking up when the telephone lines go down. This absence of technology severely limits her independence and opportunities to socialize and be safe. And did I mention it can be irritating to her family and friends? Well, that, too.

She's not the only one. If I had a nickel for every senior who bragged about how they "don't do social media" or can't understand cable or won't figure out some helpful new technology, I'd be Elon Musk rich. And it's like, why? Why wouldn't you want to stay in touch with people you love when it's a lot harder to get out of the house and be around people in older age? Why wouldn't you want to have a platform to connect and share life's happy moments with others? All the activities and relationships humans have enjoyed pursuing over the decades still exist today – the only things that have changed are the tools and venues used to practice them.

I get it. It takes work to learn new things. Humans, as a rule, also don't like change. But your family, friends, and community are too important to ignore.

Luckily, the trends are looking pretty good for senior technology use, and for God's sake, please do your best to be part of the uptick. The pandemic helped change the trajectory, and that is a big win. A 2021 research report from AARP found that more older adults (44 percent) view technology more positively as a way to stay connected than before COVID-19. Additionally, four out of five adults aged 50+ rely on technology to stay connected and in touch with family and friends. On the negative side, the report also found the greater adoption of and reliance on technology is uneven, with 15 percent of adults 50+ not having access to any internet and 60 percent saying the cost of high-speed internet is a problem.

Here are some other statistics from the study, and I share them to inspire you to geri-greatness in the high-tech department:

- Annual tech spending by the 50+ exponentially increased – from $394 to $1,144. The top three tech purchases were smartphones, smart TVs, and earbuds/Bluetooth headsets.

- Using technology to connect with others across multiple forms of communication has increased since the onset of the pandemic. Many say they are using video chats (45%), texting (37%), emailing (26%), and phones (29%) more now than before the pandemic. As of 2019, about half had never used video chat, but by 2020, 70% had, with 1 in 3 using video chat weekly.

- Tech use among the 50+ increased, particularly in wearable devices – from 17% to 27%.

- 50+ use of smartphones increased dramatically. For instance, use for ordering groceries grew from 6% to 24%; use for personal health increased from 28% to 40% for activities like telehealth visits, collecting prescriptions, or making appointments; use for health and fitness information increased from 25% to 44%; and use for financial transactions increased 37% to 53%.

- Half of the 50+ want to learn more about using tech (54%).

- Cost (38%), awareness/lack of knowledge (37%), and privacy concerns (34%) are the top self-reported barriers holding the 50+ back from adopting new technology.

- Privacy concerns remain a factor in tech, with 83% lacking confidence that what they do online remains private.

- Weekly use of streaming increased to 58% from 44%, a significant shift in how the 50+ consume entertainment.

- Shifts in technology are happening! Just as they have through the decades – even in "the good old days" when we were using cord phones, Apple 2E mainframes, and floppy disks.

No one in my life illustrated this tenet better than my mom's Dad, Charles "Woodsy" aka "Pampaw" Harper. Let me be clear: he could be an angry, OCD little fella and be meticulous and unwavering — but he sure did see the value in keeping up with current events and technology. He was among the first to buy a big a** microwave, and no one was EVER allowed to stand in front of it. And speaking of big a**, you should've seen the size of the concrete satellite dish he installed at our farm and the 20 pounds of technology in his early model cordless phone and television sets, the ones that kept him relevant and educated about the day's stock news and politics — the ones he would yell at until his face was a cherry red. He was fluent in CB radio, VCR buttons, and cassette players. He and my grandmother lived four blocks away, but Pampaw's determination to stay current with communication and entertainment technology made staying connected much more accessible for my mom. And it was all positive, as long as you didn't try to talk to him during the news.

Ready to be like Pampaw? Down with setting your satellite to tech-savvy? Here are a few keys to better floppy disk functionality:

- Start with the basics of user-friendly, intuitive devices like smartphones or tablets.

- Watch tutorials online – you can learn a lot from YouTube videos.

- Ask the young people you know to come over and teach you how to do all the things. Pay them big money.

- Sign up for a technology workshop.

- See what the library can offer you.

- Seriously, sign up for social media and practice sharing and posting daily.

- Stay informed about technology-related trends.

- Be patient, practice, and stay the course.

- Don't be a victim – know the ins and outs of cybersecurity.

The bottom line is don't stress about mastering it – don't worry about being imperfect in your execution or embrace of technology. No one knows how it works. No one. And no one is a perfect executor of it. Keep your toes in the water, stay relevant, and be a connected geri-person.

Helpful resources:

The Older Person's Guide to New Stuff by Mark Leigh

Old Age: A Beginners Guide by Michael Kinsley

AARP TEK (Technology Education & Knowledge) Academy

My iPad for Seniors Series, by Michael Miller

SeniorNet.org: SeniorNet

YouTube tutorials for seniors: There are many YouTube channels dedicated to teaching seniors about technology. Channels like "Tech Boomers," "Ask a Tech Teacher," and "EasyTechSeniors" provide step-by-step tutorials on using smartphones, computers, social media platforms, and other digital tools.

STEP 16: INVEST RESOURCES IN YOUNGER GENERATIONS, SERVICE, OTHERS.

THE PROBLEM, IN REAL **talk:**

This issue is somewhat related to earlier "steps" like lessening self and accepting age and state. And this isn't a problem as much as an opportunity. Redirecting focus toward young people we love and organizations, communities, and people who might benefit from our support is a tangible, practical, and transforming act. Being a mentor and community service volunteer is the highest and best use of self and affects the highest return. Support ourselves with a new shoe collection, and we get a momentary lift. Support younger loved ones and service initiatives, and you lift up lives. This is real purchasing power, whether it's sharing wisdom, presence, time, or treasure. We need more life-changing, legacy-building advancement in our wallets as we age. Less self, more selflessness.

The solution IMHO:

Mentor younger people and apply your strengths to service work. It's that simple.

In a 2019 article in "Greater Good Magazine," author Marc Freedman explains the critical nature of intergenerational interactions.

"As I recount in my new book *How to Live Forever: The Enduring Power of Connecting the Generations,* when younger and older connect, the intergenerational relationships built are a route to success in early life and a key to happiness and well-being in our later years."

That's a powerful promise! Freedman suggests six ways to better connect with younger people, including combining purpose and a paycheck, getting proximate, listening up, finding creative ways to connect, and living on by letting go. The "listen up" suggestion was my favorite and bears a quick share of Freedman's thoughts. "One of my mentors, John Gardner – Lyndon Johnson's Secretary of Health, Education and Welfare and a remarkable social entrepreneur – used to talk about how easy and seductive it is to be interesting. The much harder but more worthwhile trait is being interested. Young people want mentors who are focused on listening more than talking."

According to a 2009 study from Washington University's Center for Social Development, the results of this connection work have teeth.

"Tutors over 55 who help young students regularly experience physical and mental health outcomes, according to studies released by researchers at Washington University in St. Louis and Johns Hopkins University School of Medicine. The tutors studied were members of Experience Corps. This award-winning organization trains thousands of people over 55 to tutor children in urban public schools across the country," the study brief read.

This doesn't mean you have to go out and join a particular intergenerational tutoring program, volunteer at a school, or become a teacher. Relationships with younger people can be found in your backyard or down the street. You may have younger children, grandchildren, or special friends who could benefit from more time and direction from you. Your unique experiences and support can enrich a younger person's life! The time is now to get off that wallet, away from me-centered thinking, and make a difference in the lives of younger loved ones.

You won't be alone in your spending. An April 2019 study from AARP suggested grandparents spend approximately $179 billion per year on their grandchildren, roughly $2,562 per grandparent, on everything from gifts to education to experiences.

"The AARP survey revealed that while grandparents make important financial contributions to their grandchildren, they share wisdom and guidance. Many say they relish advising on everything from health to education, thereby providing a moral compass and emotional and social support. Grandparents also contribute to their grandchildren's well-being by babysitting or by acting as their primary caregivers. One in ten lives in the same household as their grandchildren and babysit, and 5% of grandparents provide their grandchildren's primary care, according to the nationally representative sample. A strong majority (73%) of the grandparents surveyed enjoy their role and rate their performance as high, up from 66% in 2011," the AARP study report read.

I have many fond memories from trips my grandparents sponsored when I was a teenager. They were rabid Love Boat fans, and, as such, they took us on Princess cruises all over the world – from Hawaii to Norway to the Caribbean. We saw so much! They also squirrelled money away to help pay for college and life beyond. They babysat us occasionally and maintained a weekend retreat outside of town so we could all be together in peace and quiet most weekends. These investments made a difference! They shaped my life in significant ways!

But I also appreciate the little – no-cost – ways they influenced our lives. I remember learning a lot about life watching the evening news with them, and later "Dallas" and "Fantasy Island" while my grandmother scratched my back and told me how I had the driest skin she'd ever touched and did I want some Lubriderm. My other grandmother supported us with fresh socks from Bill's Dollar Store and handwritten scripture sent through the mail. She made us goulash when she came to visit, she prayed for us and took us to church. Those also were incredibly meaningful acts.

So, as you think of ways to connect with and inspire your younger people, start with the free stuff – and dedicate yourself to it; this is such significant work.

Active volunteerism is another pathway to self- and community improvement. Plus – come on, everybody's doing it! (lol) According to the Bureau of Labor Statistics, in 2015, among the U.S. civilian population ages 16 and over, 63 million people, or 25 percent, volunteered. Among people ages 65 and over, 11 million volunteered, or about 24 percent of the population in that age group. Although its volunteer rate was about the same as that of the total population, the older population accounted for median annual hours of volunteering that were close to double the median for the total population ages 16 and over. Overall, most volunteers combined paid work with volunteer work; however, for the older population, three-quarters of the volunteers were not in the paid labor force.

The Corporation for National and Community Service (CNCS), the federal agency responsible for the nation's volunteer and service efforts, released a report in 2019 indicating consistent volunteering can improve the health and well-being of people 55 and older.

"The study examined how participation in national service contributes to changes in health and well-being of Senior Corps volunteers in the Senior Companion and Foster Grandparent programs—who help home-bound seniors maintain independence and tutor and mentor at-risk youth, respectively. A companion study explored the health benefits to caregivers who receive support from Senior Corps Senior Companion volunteers. According to the research, Senior Corps volunteers report much higher self-rated health scores, which is considered a valid marker of actual health, compared to older adults in similar circumstances who do not volunteer. They also reported feeling significantly less depressed and isolated compared to non-volunteers."

Other findings include:

- After two years of service in Senior Corps, 84 percent of older adults reported improved or stable health.

- 32 percent of Senior Corps volunteers who reported good health at the beginning of the study reported improved health at the two-year follow-up.

- Of those who reported five or more symptoms of depression at the beginning of the study, 78 percent said they felt less depressed two years later.

- 88 percent of Senior Corps volunteers who first described a lack of companionship reported a decrease in feelings of isolation after two years.

- Among those who initially reported a lack of companionship, 71 percent reported an improvement in their companionship status.

Ready to get involved? The website volunteermatch.org is a great place to start finding community service opportunities in your community. But you don't have to dig too deep. Sometimes, the answers are right there in front of you at your church, at the school down the street, or with a next-door neighbor in need. There are many people in need just outside our doors if we take a minute to see them.

When we participate in more do-unto-others-type activities, we lose focus on ourselves and all those boring non-issues that bring us down. Then, magically, life starts getting better. Helping and mentoring others is another key to grand-planning success.

Helpful Resources:

The Mentor's Guide: Facilitating Effective Learning Relationships, by Lois J. Zachary.

MENTOR: The National Mentoring Partnership

The Art of Being a Healing Presence: A Guide for Those in Caring Relationships, by James E. Miller:

Big Brothers Big Sisters of America

Experience Corps AARP

STEP 17: PLAY THE "WHAT IF" GAME CONSTANTLY, GET MENTALLY PREPARED.

T HE PROBLEM, IN REAL **talk:**

We need to better prepare for all the senior curve balls coming our way and have closed our eyes to the realities of their existence. Therefore, we are terrible contingency planners, constantly facing unexpected crises that result in horrible, last-minute decisions.

The solution IMHO:

Here's another easy answer. This time, it's simply playing the "What-If" game like your life depends on it.

Trust me, this is a much better game than the alternatives, "What Now?" or "What Did You THINK Was Going to Happen?" which are traumatizing games that require zero strategy and yield no winners. In "What-If," you are in a pole position when you can answer or consider questions like "What if I become incapacitated but am otherwise healthy and lucid for decades, how will I cover my care costs, and where would I live?" Or "What if I develop dementia, how can I mitigate its impact on myself and others, and how much will that cost?" Or "What if I am no longer mobile; how will I maintain my independence and what tools, resources, and savings will I need to keep chugging along in my own special way?"

There are so many rabbit holes and complicated questions — but so much panic is averted for all when you at least play the game and start the conversation and strategy-building.

Helpful Resources:

Your Complete Guide to a Successful & Secure Retirement, by Larry Swedroe and Kevin Grogan.

Eldercare Locator

AARP Roadmap for the Rest of Your Life: Smart Choices About Money, Health, Work, Lifestyle... and Pursuing Your Dreams, by Bart Astor.

Medicare.gov

Step 18: Play "Ask Yourself, Honestly," plan authentically for your future.

THE PROBLEM, IN REAL **talk:**

The older we get, the harder it is to accept the realities of who we are, what makes us happy, and how our preferences, resources, and abilities factor into the geri-planning equation.

I know a lovely, physically able, socially active senior who is hell-bent on living in a smallish house he is remodeling for an "age in place" future. This is all well and good:

- He can afford the maintenance costs to live there.

- It's a familiar neighborhood close to friends and family.

- He has sound plans on how to self-pay for future in-home care costs.

- He has made critical structural changes to the home to accommodate any physical challenges that may present as he ages.

He has really done his homework, and this is impressive.

Though thoughtful in his planning, he has not been candid about one critical, hugely influential factor: he thrives on socializing. He loves seeing people, making plans, and being out and about with friends and family, and he struggles deeply with FOMO, a fear of missing out. He is an extroverted extrovert—an anti-loner. Of course, he can flex this strength all day long in his age-in-place home, but what happens when he and his friends who "don't do technology" can't drive anymore? What then? What happens when he wants to run into people now and again but can't because of that dang hip? What then?

He is the kind of person who can figure that out, so I'm not worried about his future. But I wish he had considered his "people personality" before throwing money at his house. Because a nice condominium tower – an elevator ride away from the friends in his social circles and a scooter ride away from the grocery store and public park – may have been the better ticket. It may be hard to admit, but when we're honest about who we are, we can be better advocates for ourselves and our futures.

Not thinking or planning with authenticity at the forefront can cause you to fall into some deep potholes on the sunset stroll. When you aren't asking yourself questions like "Can I afford it?" or "Can I physically or emotionally manage it?" or, more to the point, "Does it bring me joy?" you are doing yourself – and your loved ones – a tremendous disservice.

The solution IMHO:

In the last chapter, we discussed the importance of playing the "What If?" game like your life depends on it — which it does – which is why we should all be playing it fervently as we move into our geri-years. In this game, players are challenged to talk about how they will handle crazy, out-of-the-blue, previously unconsidered, often scary scenarios that may manifest during the sunset stroll — emergencies like, say, you have a stroke and you become immobile, and you're still living in your three-story mansion with all your pretty, heavy, unmarketable things and you need 24-7 care stat and how will you pay for this and what will you do? Seriously, what would you do if that happens? What happens if you've had too many fender benders and the doctor, or your concerned and irritated children, says, "Nope, no more driving for you." What if you have to give up the keys? There are no rules or strategies to "What If?" but you win if you flex your contingency planning strengths. You win when your brain is better prepared for the unknowns and surprises that are ALWAYS lurking on that path to Golden Year greatness.

But if you're bored with (or scared by!) that game, I have another one for you. It's called "Ask Yourself, Honestly." It's for one or more players. You can play when you wake up at 3 a.m. cursing the clock or when you're two glasses into a lovely chard at the Thanksgiving dinner table. It's an anybody, anywhere, all welcome, anything goes contest. Sure to please! This is arguably a much easier game because the correct answers are at the tip of your tongue and easily accessible in the fat, healthy parts of your temporal lobe. You'll be a BIG WINNER in this game if you know yourself. "Ask Yourself, Honestly" has one objective: to build a healthy "I know myself" attitude to help inform long-term planning.

I'll play, and you'll catch on quick, promise. I'm guaranteed to win, and so are you.

Question: Are you an introvert or an extrovert?

Me/Answer: I am an introvert.

Question: Do you enjoy gardening and mowing the lawn?

Me/Answer: No, I do not. I'm not too fond of it.

Question: Do you enjoy seeing people and being included in casual events?

Me/Answer: Yes, I do. Who wouldn't?

Question: What is your vision of residential living in Northeast Florida?

Me/Answer: To live somewhere with a view of the water.

Question: Do you like living in Northeast Florida? Is this your long-term town?

Me/Answer: Actually, it is. My friends, family, and community are here, and I love being part of it.

Question: Are you likely to call a friend or family member if you are sick, sad, or need little human interaction/sympathy?

Me/Answer: No, I am not. I am happy to blog about it but will likely keep my GD needs to myself, sulking about it and mirror-talking to myself over it all the while.

Question: Does hosting your children and family make you happy?

Me/Answer: Yes, it does, duh.

Ding! Ding! Ding! I am a winner! A big winningest winner! I am my own reigning champ of "Ask Yourself, Honestly." And here's what my most honest championship-level answers reveal about my best planning practices for geri-living: I will be happiest, safest, and most content in a three-bedroom, St. Johns riverfront condominium community, where I can accommodate visiting family, be close to family and friends, and live near people who can check on me and inquire about me and invite me to play fun games like Mahjong. I won't have to pull weeds and complain about how gross and rooty our yard looks. This vision makes me happy, which is a good sign about this long-term strategy's success and staying power.

The best part of "Ask Yourself, Honestly" is you can play for years and enrich your outcomes greatly. Plus, there's the added wisdom of playing with friends and family, so they can remind you of your answers when it's time to put the deposit down on that riverfront condo, the one with the sweeping views of the river and downtown Jacksonville, the one that is just an elevator ride away from Mahjong.

Harvard Medical School's Harvard Health Publishing shared an article highlighting "6 Ways You Can Prepare to Age Well." As you might expect, this article had some really good information. I turned their six very astute suggestions into questions that could help you win in the next round of honest asking:

- How can your home be adapted?

- How can you prevent falls?

- What are your housing options?

- How are you going to get the help you need?

- How can you think ahead about getting the help you need?

- How will you plan for emergencies?

- What will your advance directives include?

Good luck with your geri-question gaming. I hope you win!

Helpful Resources:

Necessary Conversations: Between Adult Children And Their Aging Parents, by Gerald Kaufman, L.C.S.W. and L.I.S.W. and Sarah M. Tolson.

The 36-Hour Day: A Family Guide to Caring for People Who Have Alzheimer's Disease, Other Dementias, and Memory Loss, by Nancy L. Mace and Peter V. Rabins.

Being Mortal: Medicine and What Matters in the End, by Atul Gawande.

Aging Life Care Association: Aging Life Care Professionals, formerly known as Geriatric Care Managers, specialize in helping seniors and their families navigate the complexities of aging.

Designing Your Life: How to Build a Well-Lived, Joyful Life, by Bill Burnett and Dave Evans.

STEP 19: BE REALISTIC, OPEN AND FLEXIBLE.

THE PROBLEM, IN REAL **talk:**

Anyone who's been a caregiver or managed support for an elderly loved one knows this problem well. It is punctuated by comments like, "I'm never going into assisted living" or "I don't need _____ (fill in the blank – hearing aids, adult diapers, walker, help with bathing, etc.) Or it comes in the form of complaints like "I don't like that nurse because _____," or "the food there is terrible," or "That place is for old people." Sometimes, it is best described as profound reluctance, like "I'll never understand that social media," "If I can't drive, I can't do anything anymore," or "This landline is the only communication tool I need." It includes a little something from every chapter so far because being unrealistic, closed off, and inflexible are the roots of geri-drama in all forms.

The solution IMHO

Sharpen your resilience – start today and practice it often. Not only will this make managing your senior years easier for yourself and your loved ones, but it is also highly beneficial to your health and wellness.

A 2016 study from Geriatric Nursing bears this out. The results reveal it's something we can all work on and improve as we age. "Resilience is most often viewed as a process rather than a personality trait; as such, many older adults are capable of improving their resilience later in life. The key characteristics of highly resilient individuals have been demonstrated in various studies and include mental, social, and physical factors that lead to optimal outcomes of improved quality of life, happiness, and well-being as well as reduced depression."

A May 2023 article in the American Seniors Housing Association's "Where You Live Matters" blog includes helpful, achievable suggestions on strengthening resilience during the senior stroll. The piece outlines a workout plan that any one of us can accomplish:

- Maintain an optimistic attitude and always look for the "silver lining."

- Engage in new activities.

- Cultivate new friendships or join a social group.

- Accept that some things are out of your control and take action on the things you can affect.

- Practice stress-management techniques.

- Develop a spiritual practice like prayer, meditation, yoga, or mindful journaling.

- Maintain perspective; don't let your thoughts run away with you.

- Practice self-care through proper nutrition, regular exercise, and good sleep habits.

- Volunteer your time to help others.

- Ask for help when you need it.

- Look for the lessons you can learn from the situation.

All of these suggestions from the "Where You Live Matters" article are a compilation of solutions from prior chapters and suggest how foundational being open, flexible, and realistic is to a workable grand plan. This gets to the heart of our geri-everything!

Cultivating flexibility and adaptability is essential because it can lead to a more fulfilling and contented senior experience. Don't we all want some of that? The path along which we saunter through our golden years is full of potholes – you can see most of them from great distances if you take those gd blinders off and look ahead – early and often. As smartly trained athletes stretch before setting out on a long run or a challenging workout, we can hone our flexibility for the challenges and changes that define most ordinary people's older adulthood.

Flexibility will help us medal in:

- Physical changes, so we can adapt, get good medical care, and adopt new strategies for well-being

- Changing social circles so we can form new relationships and socially engage as friends and family members move away, pass on, or become less available

- Transitions in work or careers so we can find new interests, hobbies, or volunteer efforts that inspire us

- Adjustments to living arrangements so we can live in places that suit our changing physical and social needs and redefine our sense of community

- Emotional coping skills so we won't be so stressed and cray-cray!

- Staying connected and embracing technology so we can keep up with our loved ones and the people who make up our community

- Travel and exploring so we can see new people, places, and things

- Learning new stuff so we can contribute to our sense of personal growth, brain function, and intellect

- Positive thinking, so we can see changes and challenges as opportunities for growth and new joy

Being flexible, open, and realistic is the bottom line for successful grand planning – right next to being communicative and trusting of those who love and help us. When we can embrace all the changes that come our way with an open mind, some transitions aren't such a big deal. We don't have to be a rock in the stream or a stick in the mud whenever we stumble into one of those sunset stroll potholes we all should have seen coming. Instead, we can see them on the horizon and skip toward them with a positive attitude and sense of purpose.

Helpful Resources:

Who Moved My Cheese?, by Spencer Johnson.

The Obstacle Is the Way: The Timeless Art of Turning Trials into Triumph, by Ryan Holiday.

Online learning platforms like Coursera and edX offer various courses on various subjects, including personal development and adaptability skills.

Embracing Uncertainty: Breakthrough Methods for Achieving Peace of Mind When Facing the Unknown, by Susan Jeffers.

STEP 20: DESIGN A LEGACY THAT YOU'LL BE PROUD OF, PRACTICE EMPATHY, HUMILITY AND GRATITUDE.

THE PROBLEM, IN REAL **talk:**

I have heard it said over and over again — sometimes in this venue and many times from my own mouth — how negative experiences and non-Grand-Planning can reframe, mar, or even wreck a loved one's once legacy.

And by legacy, I'm not talking about financial planning and wills and what you're leaving to whom. I'm talking about how you're remembered when you're gone – what strengths defined you and which ones stand out in the memories of your loved ones. Is your legacy one of unconditional love, generosity, and graciousness – or one of worry, emotional disconnect, and antagonism?

In Michael Hebb's *Let's Talk about Death (over Dinner): An Invitation and Guide to Life's Most Important Conversation*, one of the conversation prompts is "What kind of legacy do you wish to leave?" This is such a critical thought! It's different for all of us, but who wants to pursue a legacy that is negatively charged, deplorable, or so painful no one wants to remember it?

The problem with legacy-building is that our actions sometimes need to align with the vision as we age. I've heard so many people talk about this phenomenon with their parents or elderly friends. Empathy, humility, and gratitude seem to fade during the golden years, resulting in relationships that can be annoyingly one-sided and unsatisfying.

I dare you to visit a caregiver support group on the Facebook and hear how people's lives are altered in this role. These caregivers have their lives on hold for their loved ones. Many of them are desperate, angry, and fed up because there is such a shortage of gratitude and empathy from their senior loved ones.

I know firsthand how legacies can be marred by negative caregiving situations. The older woman I helped during her final months was, for many years, a second mother to me. She's part of my earliest memories. An OG working mom, she had high standards and gave generously of herself to create opportunities for others. She was a warm hugger, called you honey and meant it, and she was inventive, wise, and principled. After my caregiving experience with her, those memories were reduced to angry reflections. Now, what I remember about her is all the stuff, the unfinished business, the refusals to reason, and the unwelcome stress that seeped – actually, fire-hosed – into my life.

The majority of Americans don't want this kind of legacy, according to a study published on AARP's website in 2019. The 2019 poll by BMO Wealth Management showed most people have better intentions.

The survey of 502 Americans over 55 found that "a majority – 54 percent – of older Americans want to be remembered for their values and the life lessons they've shared with family and friends. That's far more than the 31 percent who mentioned a family business as part of their legacy," the AARP article summarized. "Some 29 percent said they wanted to be remembered for charitable acts and donations, while 28 percent wanted their name associated with public service or community involvement. Only 1 in 4 – 26 percent – said they wanted to be remembered for the personal possessions and financial assets they've accumulated."

Yet people need to plan for it! The other factor influencing legacy-making is a general reluctance to grand plan. This is a significant issue today, as people generally experience the hardships of loss and eldercare management later in life – people are living longer, and you don't think about grand planning until you've experienced it! According to a 2019 study from Merrill Lynch and Age Wave called "Leaving a Legacy: A Lasting Gift to Loved Ones," which was profiled in a February 15, 2019, *Forbes* magazine article, nearly half of Americans over the age of 55 do not have a will in place. Yet, most people know it's something they need to address. The same study said most people know they should "have their affairs in order" by age 50, and 69 percent want to leave a positive legacy for their families. So people see this legacy planning as necessary – but about half of us haven't even started working on it!

When we are ill-prepared for the golden years and fail to develop and maintain a plan for our legacies, panic sets in, and our sense of self inflates. That leaves less room for our carefully curated humility, empathy, and gratitude qualities. This darkens even the best-made plans – challenging relationships and leaving prized legacies withering on the vine.

The solution IMHO:

With a bit of Grand Plan-ing and self-awareness, we can prune destructive thinking and behaviors and design legacies that are meaningful to everyone.

The first step is where a lot of self-help books begin: the act of practicing gratitude. In a December 2022 "Speaking of Health" article, Mayo Clinic Health System suggests being grateful on the daily and keeping a gratitude journal – "just as you'd take that magic pill if it existed."

"Try starting your day by thinking of someone you're grateful for as soon as you wake up. It could be appreciating a friend who sends you funny texts, a teacher who recognizes your child's gifts, or the barista who hands you your coffee and shares friendly conversation. Later, thank that person with a text, note, or kind word when you see the person," the article stated.

Being grateful changes our biology by releasing the oxytocin hormone into our system. This helps us connect with people – a really good thing for building a legacy of love!

"Set aside some time during your day, perhaps while attempting to relax your mind before sleep. Think back on your day and write down the things that went right. Maybe your spouse took care of a household repair, you heard your favorite song on the radio, or you saw a double rainbow. Try writing about the many blessings you may have taken for granted, such as having clean water or having certain abilities," the Mayo article suggested.

The next step is to address our empathy and humility, which usually come hand-in-hand. When you're showing empathy, you're humbled – and vice-versa. We teach our children these basic lessons from their earliest years, whether through thank-you note-writing nudges or time-out sessions that begin with questions like "Just who do you think you are?" or "How do you think that made someone feel?" We need a refresher course on these essential topics later in life. And it's not too late. According to a May 2016 *Huffington Post* article by writer, trainer, and speaker Anne Loehr, we can build empathy with these seven practical tips:

- Listen and don't interrupt.

- Be fully present with people and tune in to non-verbal communication.

- Smile at people.

- Use people's names and encourage them.

- Try to empathize with people whose beliefs you don't share.

- Give genuine recognition.

- Challenge yourself to have a deeper conversation.

The last step in legacy building is to treat your legacy as a nonprofit organization might treat its mission statement. Decide how you want to be remembered and stick to your brand and mission. For example, if you want to be remembered as generous, spend quality time with the people you love and treat them to memorable experiences or gifts of time, talent, or treasure. If your legacy planning is inspired by compassion and affection, make sure you're always sharing big bosomy hugs and notes of affirmation or encouragement.

The time is now to fertilize our legacies with self-awareness and good grand planning! We must refuse to let obstinance, poor preparation, and ego reduce us to a pitiful portrayal of how NOT to be.

When I'm a super-fly, super-fine senior, I want to be aware that my behavior, situation, or condition could — and probably aready IS —significantly affect(ing) someone else's life. Please, Lord, do not let me go through my golden years oblivious to the truth that helping me probably means someone loving is giving up their lunch hour, vacation, paycheck, career, family time, or future vision. Please remind me to be grateful, always.

Helpful Resources:

Ethical Wills & How to Prepare Them: A Guide to Sharing Your Values from Generation to Generation, by Barry K. Baines.

Legacy Letters Workbook: A Step-by-Step Guide to Writing a Legacy Letter.

Family tree and genealogy websites like Ancestry.com: Researching family history and creating a detailed family tree can provide valuable insights that document family lineage, stories, and photographs.

The Last Lecture, by Randy Pausch and Jeffrey Zaslow.

Helpful Resources

THE GENTLE ART OF Swedish Death Cleaning, Margareta Magnusson

The Swedish Art of Aging Exuberantly, Margareta Magnusson

Mothercare, Lynne Tillman

The Gift of Years, Joan Chittister

Breaking the Age Code, Becca Levy

Happy Go Lucky, David Sedaris

Being Mortal, Atul Gawande

Recipes for a Sacred Life, Rivvy Neshama

How to Care for Aging Parents, Virginia Morris

Stupid Things I Won't Do When I Get Old, Steven Petrow

Getting Real About Getting Older, Linda Stroh

Lighter: Let Go of the Past, Connect with the President and Expand the Future, Yung Pueblo

I've Got Some Good News and Some Bad News: You're Old, David Bernstein

Working Daughter: A Guide to Caring for Your Aging Parents While Making a Living, Liz O'Donnell

I Feel Bad About My Neck, I Remember Nothing and Heartburn, Nora Ephron

Honest Aging: An Insider's Guide to the Second Half of Life, Rosanne M. Leipzig

Two Old Broads: Stuff You Need to Know But Didn't Know You Needed To, Dr. M.E. Hecht

How Not to Be Old (Even if You Are), Jill Orr

The Happiness Hypothesis, Jonathan Haidt

Growing Old: Notes on Aging with Something Like Grace, Elizabeth Marshall Thomas

The Book About Getting Older, Lucy Pollock

I'm Glad My Mom Died, Jeanette McCurdy

The Inner Work of Age, Connie Zweig

The 36-hour Day, A Family Guide to Caring for People Who Have Alzheimer Disease and Other Dementias, by Nancy L. Mace and Peter V. Rabins

The Happiness Project: Or, Why I Spent a Year Trying to Sing in the Morning, Clean My Closets, Fight Right, Read Aristotle and Generally Have More Fun, Gretchen Rubin

Knocking on Heaven's Door: The Path to a Better Way of Death, Katy Butler

The Art of Dying Well, Katy Butler

When Your Aging Parent Needs Help, Leslie Kernisan and Paula Spencer Scott

Mom and Dad, We Need to Talk: How to Have Essential Conversations With Your Parents About Their Finances, Cameron Huddleston

What to Do When I'm Gone, A Mother's Wisdom to Her Daughter, Suzy Hopkins and Hallie Bateman

Let's Talk About Death Over Dinner, Michael Hebb

From Strength to Strength: Finding Success, Happiness and Deep Purpose in the Second Half of Life, Arthur C. Brooks

The Five Wishes, Aging With Dignity

The Book of Charlie: Wisdom from the Remarkable American Life of a 109-year-old Man, David Von Drehle

How Will You Measure Your Life? Clayton Christensen

Falling Into Grace: Insights on the End of Suffering, Adyashanti

Heartwood: The Art of Living with the End in Mind, Barbara Becker

The Celestine Prophecy, by James Redfield

Necessary Conversations: Between Families and Their Aging Parents, by Gerald Kaufman

Boundaries Updated and Expanded Edition: When to Say Yes, How to Say No To Take Control of Your Life, by Henry Cloud

How to Retire Happy, Wild, and Free: Retirement Wisdom That You Won't Get from Your Financial Advisor, by Ernie J. Zelinski

Dying Well: Peace and Possibilities at the End of Life, by Ira Byock MD

Yours Truly: An Obituary Writer's Guide to Telling Your Story, by James R. Hagerty

Final Rights: Reclaiming the American Way of Death, by Joshua Slocum

Heartfelt Memorial Services: Your Guide for Planning Meaningful Funerals, Celebrations of Life and Times of Remembrance, by Beverly Molander

The Good Death: An Exploration of Dying in America, by Ann Neumann

Before I Go: The Essential Guide to Creating a Good End of Life Plan, by Jane Duncan Rogers

GRAND PLANNER

I F YOU WERE INSPIRED by the real talk encouragement in Grand Plans, make your preparations a reality by completing the Grand Planner — a workbook pairing for Grand Plans: How to Mitigate Geri-Drama in 20 Easy Steps. Grand Planner is available in local bookstores, Amazon and through the Grand Plans website at www.mygrandplans.com. Time to get planning!

The Grand Plans Semimonthly
Substack Newsletter

S IGN UP TODAY FOR a semi-monthly newsletter from Grand Plans designed to normalize and celebrate our glorious geri-destiny through information, stories, real talk conversation, smart planning and shared experience. Subscribe at https://susannabarton.substack .com

Author Bio

Susanna P. Barton

Susanna Barton self-publishes Lenten challenges each year and 2024's will be taking the "I" out of Lent, because it's Lent, not lint. Look out for *Rolling My I-s: A Lenten Challenge to Give Up Me, Myself & I-Talk*, coming out this year! You can find her offerings at www.givingitupforlent.com. When it's not Lent, she enjoys stirring healthy conversations about aging and being prepared for it. Founder of the Grand Plans online community (@MyGrandPlans on Facebook, @GrandPlans2022 on Instagram and @GrandPlans on YouTube) and host of the podcast "Grand Plans," Barton also maintains a website where she blogs and curates information, stories and tools about geri-drama and planning for our sunset stroll. (www.mygrandplans.com). This year, she was appointed to Jacksonville Mayor Donna Deegan's subcommittee on eldercare issues to help older adults in the community access senior resources. A graduate of Hollins College in Roanoke, VA, Barton has written and edited professionally for *The Austin Business Journal, The Jacksonville Business Journal* and *The Resident*, a monthly newspaper in Jacksonville FL for which she writes a popular column on gratitude. Barton also has provided content and articles for several nonprofit organizations during her 30-year writing career including the Community Foundation for Northeast Florida Jacksonville University and The Bolles School, where she worked for 10 years in corporate communications. An empty-nester and mother of two awesome grown-and-flown 20-somethings, Ben and Marley, Susanna and her husband, David, live in Florida with their geri-dog, Dot, and sometimes their grandkitten, Bean (short for Bean & Cheese Taco).

Made in United States
Troutdale, OR
09/16/2024

22862301R00076